D1050574

Social Media Marketing

Step by Step Instructions For Advertising Your Business on Facebook, Youtube, Instagram, Twitter, Pinterest, Linkedin and Various Other Platforms [2nd Edition]

The trademarks are used without consent, and the publication of the trademark is without permission or backing by the trademark owner. All trademarks and brands within this book are for clarification purposes only and are owned by the owners themselves and not affiliated with this document.

Table of Contents

Introduction

We all love to use social media for various reasons. We go online to send photos to other people, to let people know where we are or just to chat in general. Social media has truly evolved to where people can do practically anything online. However, social media is not only for communicating about random subjects with other people.

Today, social media is used for a business to market anything. It is possible to go to any social media platform and interact with others by talking about your business and what you- sell or promote. You can let others know everything you want to do while encouraging people to see that your business is one they can trust.

All kinds of businesses have their own social media handles. They use them to tell people about unique things they offer. Sometimes they use social media just to interact with their customers. Social media is all about getting in touch with the people companies rely upon. You can do the same for your own business too.

You will have to target audiences on social media to make your business stand out. People are flocking to social media sites like never before. Those individuals know that social media offers more information on things of their interest. Use social media to make your work more visible and explain what makes your work attractive if people are to pay attention to you.

To make it all work, it is imperative that you know how to get onto social media sites and how to use them. This guide will provide you the details to get the most out of your social media efforts.

This guide includes information on all major social media sites available, and what to do with them. Facebook is the best option to utilize for your marketing plans however, to be well informed, read about various other social media platforms. These include Twitter, Instagram, and many others that target specific groups of people.

Each section in this guide will help you understand what makes each social media platform special. You will be able to decide which ones you need to target and then learn how to reach people through each of those platforms. This will give you a sense of control when you work online.

The types of advertisements to produce for your site are extensive. You can work video ads, photo ads, and many others. Points on how to produce unique advertisements and listings are included in this guide.

Some of the social media marketing solutions to utilize entail paid advertising. This is where you pay a social media site to make your messages more noticeable. It is not essential that you use paid advertising, but this guide will help you understand how the process works. It could help you to have more exposure on social media or make something that is working online even more efficient and viable.

Every social media platform is different in various ways. Discover how each social media option works and how you can leverage them to your benefit.

All of the social media sites will work for various users on desktop and mobile devices alike. With so many social media sites working with mobile apps, it only makes sense that you target people who have those devices. In fact, some social media sites focus exclusively on mobile users. This guide will help you to target people regardless of what device they are using.

The points listed in this social media marketing book will illustrate what you can get out of your business. This guide is to help you get a better chance of getting the word out about what you are marketing. It is all about standing out from the rest of the pack.

Advisory Notes

All information in this guide is accurate as of January 2018. All social media sites can alter regarding the layout of the site, the processes used for producing and hosting content and so forth. There are no guarantees that certain social media sites will remain in the future. Some of them may merge with others over time. Be attentive to any changes or additions that a social media site can use.

Each social media page has its own terms and conditions on how it operates. These include terms based on what to post, how to promote yourself, and other rules. Review these guidelines before beginning work on any social media page. Failing to follow the terms listed on a social media site could result in being banned from the site. The instructions and processes noted throughout this guide are designed with these terms in mind. Follow them precisely while implementing your best judgment when building the content for your page.

Chapter 1 – Why Social Media Marketing Is Important

You may perhaps have the best product in your industry. It could be the greatest thing ever made and would make a difference in someone's life. However, that does not mean people will see your creation. Your product or service may not have many sales. Without proper marketing, no one may notice what you offer. To let people see your products or services you need to promote your work with an extensive marketing campaign.

Marketing is one of the toughest things to do when it comes to running a business. Promoting your business will be more than just telling people about what you offer. You should let people know that you exist in the first place. It is all about letting people know that what you offer is valuable and that you are available for business.

You want people learn what your product or service is and what makes it special. Also, tell people what makes your offering worthwhile. More importantly, you need to stand out from the rest of the market. The audience needs to know why your goods or services are different from everything else.

However, don't market yourself on any outlet. You have to get online to market your business. Traditional marketing avenues are starting to dry up as newspapers, and other print forms of media are not cutting it anymore. It is a matter of time before the online world becomes the only place where people search for items of their interest.

Promoting your business online is not always easy. You need to get out there and show people that you have something useful. It is all about letting the public know what you do and what you offer them.

It is often a challenge to become visible online. You might have the best business idea in the world, but that will not suffice if you are unable to market your products appropriately.

The problem with today's economy is that many businesses offer the same things you provide. They might be getting more visitors to their sites than you might. Others got a head start on their marketing efforts and are doing much more to market themselves than you are.

Whether you plan to run an online retail shop or a physical store, you need to know how to create an online presence. One method is to use social media to your benefit.

Social media has never been more popular than it is now. With social media, people can interact with each other online. They can talk about anything in some of the world's most unique digital environments. Even more importantly, people are talking with each other about the products and services they deliver. Social media became a popular promotional tool that might be even more valuable than other traditional forms of advertising.

You have to make use of social media marketing to your advantage. It helps you highlight your business in a distinctive manner.

There are many good reasons why social media marketing has become very important. Let's look at a few of these points.

Easy to Reach

Social media has dominated the online world over the years. Today, people and businesses are entering an extensive variety of sites to highlight what they offer.

People access social media sites not only with computers but also with mobile apps on their tablets and Smartphones. Even smart television sets that connect online and video game consoles with similar links can get people online too. The number of social media services that are available on these devices has been expanding in volume as well.

In addition, you can easily access other peoples' devices thanks to those social media platforms running with their own special apps. Whether it entails a traditional computer or something smaller, people are discovering new ways to use social media wherever they go. This makes it easier for people to stay in touch and to find things while on the go. With your marketing efforts, you can ensure you will be on a variety of sites to make it simpler to be spotted.

A Diverse Layout

Social media marketing offers a diverse variety of places that target certain groups of people. No two social media platforms are alike. For instance, Instagram has become very popular with younger generations. They get on social media sites to share photos and short videos. LinkedIn has become attractive to professionals including people who might be trying to market extensive business programs or work-related endeavors.

What makes each social media site stand out is worth exploring. Twitter helps to share messages in as few characters as possible while Pinterest examines local businesses through unique virtual storefronts. The many great social media sites in the online world are worth exploring. Find out what sites are available and what makes each one different.

The specific social media sites available to market yourself will vary based on your needs, what you offer, and whom you want to contact. Pinterest is ideal for arts and crafts items but not appropriate for financial planning services, for example.

You should incorporate different strategies for each of these social media sites. These tactics vary based on how well they reach people and how you can communicate. This guide includes specifics on marketing through each of these sites.

A Preferred Way to Search

One great thing about social media is that it became a popular place to find information. Just go to a social media site, and you will probably see a search engine. This feature will help you locate different businesses relating to certain keywords throughout the site.

When you use the search engine on Facebook, you will find information on Facebook profiles relating to what you specified. Facebook does this to connect you to whatever you search for. You don't even leave the site; whatever you want is already there.

In other words, people are foregoing Google and other search engines in favor of search functions on social media sites. They know that it is easier to get in touch with people on social media. This leads to the next concept.

Localization has become a huge part of social media. When people search for things, the social media site will often give users local results first. That is, the most important results are not far from one's geographic location. This is the same as what you get from a regular search engine. Advertisers on social media can even plan their campaigns to target specific people in certain geographic areas.

Interactivity is Key

Interactivity is an important aspect when it comes to today's online world. People want to talk with others online. This includes businesses that might be promoting all sorts of things. When you access a social media site, you will do more than just tell people about your services. You will have an opportunity to talk with others. You can ask people questions or respond to their queries.

People love having others interact with them on social media. Think about all those fast food places that have their own Twitter accounts. These places often respond to people who tweet about foods they like, or to advertise their promotions. Those fast food spots love interacting because they know such interactions make them more attractive and appreciative. Whether it entails Burger King talking about some new breakfast item or Arby's inventing something new, such businesses talk about what is happening, what makes them special, and even answer questions.

Being direct with your customers is always important. When you run your business, you have to understand what consumers wish for. You must also reach out to them whenever they have questions, complaints, or compliments. Social media marketing provides an opportunity to discover what people ask for, and what interests them the most.

Always Evolving

Social media is always growing, and new outlets are introduced on a regular basis. These include places that cater to specific groups of people. For instance, the Major League Baseball sports organization formed its Infield Chatter social media system to allow baseball fans to talk about the sport, their favorite teams, and players. People can discuss the hottest stars, rising prospects, the history of the sport and so forth.

This is just one example of how social media is changing. In the future, there will be social media sites that are devoted to just about everything. There might be social media sites dedicated to people interested in arts and crafts or maybe ones that focus on certain video game consoles. Whatever the case may be, the social media field is always going to grow and change with the times.

It is impressive how the social media world works today. You will see throughout this guide that it is very easy to highlight your services to others. In particular, you will find many options for social media sites for free and paid marketing efforts. You might be surprised how easy it is to pull off a successful campaign on social media.

Chapter 2 – What Will You Get from Social Media Marketing?

A quality social media marketing campaign will make a world of difference for your business. To make social media marketing worthwhile, examine what you are doing to get a campaign to work well and stand out. Here are some of the best ways to create a great campaign.

Show Your Human Side

One of the greatest problems with trying to market your business online is that it might be a challenge to show your human side. People are not always interested in looking at plain websites. They might think that someone with an ordinary website is creating a list of products or services without being personal.

It is up to you to show people that you have a human side. With social media, you can express your views and feelings to others while assuring them that you care. You can give details why your offer is special and how they can benefit from what you are marketing.

Express your human side when on social media and people will start to follow. They will want to see what you have to say and will love you for it. More importantly, it shows that you understand the needs people have. After all, businesses cannot afford to be depicted as massive smoke-churning factories that only care about profits. The businesses that care about people will remain unwavering and popular and commonly make big profits. Sometimes a business could earn more than what the big guys' gross, but only if enough effort goes into the mix.

Improved Recognition

It is important for people to notice your brand. Your brand reflects your business, its image, what you sell, and the values you hold. Your business will succeed when your brand becomes easier to spot. Using the right social media marketing strategies will make your brand visible and unique.

As you get on social media, it becomes easier for people to identify your brand and everything you stand for. With this, you are showing people what you want to say and that you are vigilant.

Your social media profile will include things like the logo or name of your company, for starters. After that, you will post things on your page that illustrate what makes your work special and attractive. You can even talk about new developments in your business as they come along. You have full control over what you do on social media.

People who see your brand on different social media sites and hear from you regularly will be more interested in your offerings. They will note that you have something important to say. More importantly, people will have a clear understanding of what you present to them. They will know what your brand is all about and what your values are. Being recognized on social media is critical to your success.

Boost Your Brand Loyalty

Another great part of social media marketing is that it improves your brand loyalty. It is important to connect with people on social media so your audience notices what you offer. Getting in touch with them is critical to making those people loyal to your work.

Loyalty is critical to the success of any business. You must have a strong customer base that will stick with you. Social media marketing makes it simpler to grow your business and make it more viable.

Anyone who follows you on social media will pay attention to your every word. Your followers will read everything you share and interact with you in many ways. People want to hear you and see what you say. In particular, they will want to buy things from you, or hire your services.

More importantly, social media provides you with a captive audience that wants to hear about all you have to offer online. More people can learn what you are doing and what makes your business trustworthy. Your existing customer base sticks with you through posting your social media messages.

Anyone who follows you on social media knows everything about what you are doing. All your updates will go onto their feeds, and keep them informed about everything you put forward. Letting people know what you offer is vital to your success even if you are just communicating with people already loyal to your work. It is more than just about getting money from those people. It is also to establish strong relationships so that they trust you and follow your messages.

Convert More People

While social media makes it easy for you to get in touch with existing customers, you have to do more than that. You also have to reach new patrons. Stand out and give other people a reason why your trade is valuable and worth trusting.

Converting people you meet online into customers can be a challenge. It is tough encouraging people to see what you provide and why doing it is useful. No one is going to take you seriously when you are just starting out. However, with social media marketing, you will convert people quickly and effortlessly.

As you post things online through social media sites, people will want to listen to you and see what you offer. They will interact with you and read your blog posts, watch your videos, and so forth. You have to show people what makes your business stand out by appearing in the right places.

By humanizing your business, the conversions you require will be easier to attain . People like it when they see the emotions that a business wants to convey. There is also the benefit to interacting with people and answering questions, thus giving you extra help with getting your word out to more people. Don't forget about resolving any disputes or other issues people may have.

Getting onto social media is important as it helps you get onto more screens. When you learn to work with it, you will be successful converting people into being new customers that you can trust.

Bring More People to Your Website or Retail Store

Your social media sites are just a small part of what you can work with when marketing your business online. It is even more important to attract people to your regular website or any physical store you own.

Promoting yourself on social media is essential. You can always post links to your site through a social media post. The link on your profile name or icon could go to your website too. Directions on how to get to a physical location that you might have could also be included.

People will only click on your social media account links when they see something intriguing. This could bring them to either your website or to the main profile page for your social media account. That account page could also include a separate link to your site.

People will be inclined to click the link to get to your site when they see what you offer is appealing and valuable to them. They want to feel appreciated and that their values or desires matter to you. For physical businesses, they will be intrigued by what you offer and will want to know your store's location.

Keep Your Marketing Costs Down

One positive aspect of marketing on social media sites is that you will get more out of your marketing efforts. It is often a challenge to market your business because it costs money to print ads, rent out spaces or spots in papers or websites.

With social media, you will avoid all of those issues. You will get your page marketed online through a site that is free to utilize.

With your personal account you will be able to post messages online free of charge by using social media. All these messages will link to your business site. The fact that your work is relatively interactive and more human makes this part of marketing all the more useful.

If you are smart, you will not spend a penny on marketing. People will retweet, repost, or forward smart messages that you created. These messages will always include your name and a link to your social media profile. This makes it easier for you to market your work because other people are technically doing it for you.

Having people forward your messages is critical to your success. Even the smallest ideas can go viral in just a matter of hours. Just look online right now, and you will probably hear stories about some company or celebrity becoming the next big thing because of what their doings. The marketing efforts will make a world of difference if you know how to make them stand out well.

Some sites do offer paid advertising solutions. This is where you could get preferred treatment on a search based on certain keywords. You can always spend a bit of money on this although it is optional. Fortunately, in this guide you will discover the places that offer paid marketing solutions provide support to set up and run an affordable campaign.

Get On a Search Engine

You will obtain more traffic from a search engine if your website has more quality links going to and from its space. Providing that the links are unique and relevant to your original site.

Search engine optimization (SEO) is a vital aspect of running a business. With this, you can link up to different valuable keywords. As when using a search engine, work with the right keywords that are both popular and relevant to your business.

What is also interesting is that your site will appear on a search engine multiple times thanks to your social media channels. A Facebook channel will appear separately from your main website or an Instagram or YouTube channel, for instance. You can do this often as you want, but you must be aware of how each setup works.

In addition, your primary website will appear on search engines because proper links to social media pages are provided. Businesses with several social media accounts are more likely to appear on Google and other search engines than other groups. Those places are interpreted as more active and mindful of their potential customers.

The links between your social media sites and your main website are also important. Having more of these links ensures your main website will be easier for people to read and use. This is vital to your overall success as it helps your visibility on a quality search engine.

The benefits of social media marketing are strong and worth noticing. With all of this in mind, it is important to see what you can achieve from your campaign. In this guide, we will look at various social media networks to give you an idea of how to promote your business.

Chapter 3 – Choosing the Proper Social Media Site for Your Marketing Work

Throughout this guide, we will look into various options for social media sites that are useful for your marketing needs. You will look at many points relating to the multiple social media sites to consider what is effective.

Naturally, you can always work with all social media sites we list here; as many as you want to make yourself visible. Nevertheless, that does not mean every single one of them is sensible for your needs, let alone easy to use.

Every social media site is different based on whom it targets and how it is organized. Each social media site is unique. Choose carefully when planning your social media campaign. If anything, having multiple social media sites is best as it gives you the opportunity to accomplish more.

This chapter looks into individual social media sites based on what you can work with.

1. Look at the main goals you have for a social media campaign.

Decide why you are choosing social media in the first place. Maybe you want people to be more aware of your brand. Perhaps you are just trying to get more leads. Perhaps you might be trying to get people to download an app or reach your physical place of business.

The social media space you visit should be chosen based on what your goals are. Facebook is ideal if you want people to be more aware of your work. LinkedIn is perfect if you want to get leads. Snapchat is ideal if you want people to download an app.

Whatever the case, look at what you can get out of a social media site before you start working with it. See that the campaign is arranged correctly and that you have a clear understanding what social media sites are perfect for it. You should carefully examine how individual options might work with your various needs.

2. Consider the target audience you are trying to reach.

Every social media site has its own specific audience. LinkedIn has a great platform that is popular among professionals, preferably those who earn good wages. Instagram is useful for younger people and is prominent among today's millennials.

In 2015, the Pew Research Center found some interesting demographics surrounding social media sites. While this information is not definitive, it provides an idea of what to expect from certain social media sites:

- Facebook's user-base is extremely diverse. People of all kinds use Facebook - from the rich and poor to the young and old alike. It is equally popular among men and women and among black, white, Hispanic, and Asian audiences and other racial demographics.

- Women are more interested in using Pinterest. People from suburban areas are also interested in it more than others.

- LinkedIn is not only popular with wealthier people but also with those who have college degrees. People living in urban areas tend to use LinkedIn more often too.

- Younger people are more likely to use Twitter. Those living in urban areas will use it more often as well.

This is just a sampling of what you will discover about social media sites. All of these sites are different in how they attract various types of people. Experiment with different social media pages so you can potentially get something meaningful and important out of your campaign. As you will discover, be watchful how you can use multiple options for your campaign.

3. Look at how often people might interact with social media sites.

All social media sites have different standards of how often people interact with them. Facebook, Twitter, and Instagram are the most popular places where people are more likely to check every day or every other day. Meanwhile, Pinterest and LinkedIn are places where people will check on their feeds three to five times a week although some might do that more often.

A site that has people checking it often if you are trying to increase your brand recognition might be advisable. Sites where people do not check their profiles every day are good if you are trying to get leads or establish long-term connections with professionals in a field.

Knowing how people behave on social media sites is important when you want to interact with them. Make sure you find out how well and how easy you can communicate with someone on a site. This is to make it easier for you to interact with people and to share your interests.

4. Review what your competitors are doing.

Your competition will more than likely be on social media already or contemplating doing so in the future. Whatever the case might be, you have to look at what your competitors are doing.

Check the websites of your challengers to see what others are doing. Be sure to do what you can to compete with them and that your site is more distinct and unique. Doing so makes it easier for your page to stand out and be more attractive. Watch for how well your campaign is running and that you are not copying whatever other people are doing. Using the same social media sites and working with similar keywords or other posting strategies is good so long as your content is original.

You do not necessarily have to duplicate everything your opponents carry out. Be aware of what someone else is implementing so you have a clear idea of what you should do yourself. Keep your mind open throughout the process, but at least examine the accomplishments of others.

5. Think about the content you want to create.

Every social media site is different in terms of the message you work with. You can do anything on a social media page, but you need to discover what the standards are for each site:

- Tumblr, Pinterest, Snapchat, and Instagram are great if you are trying to market things with pictures. These social media sites are perfect for pictorial-based marketing.

- LinkedIn is ideal if you want to be more technical. The site is also great for people who want to share their opinions with others.

- YouTube and Snapchat are good for video content.

- Quora is appealing if you want to answer questions that people might have about a certain concept your business has.

- Twitter is useful for when you want to share news or ideas with people. Although only if you are trying to share smaller bits of data at a time.

Review the context before you choose a certain social media site. This is all about getting some control over your work and having everything laid out in a smart and valuable manner. Watch for how well you can produce this content too, so it becomes easier for you to generate something that is easy to follow and operate.

6. Look at the format of your content.

All social media sites have standards for how the content is posted. YouTube obviously focuses on videos while Instagram is about pictures. Twitter is for smaller messages while Facebook and LinkedIn allow more details about what you want to post.

Decide on what to post and how it will be illustrated. This is to give you a better approach to handle your work.

Think about the subject you will utilize as well. Some businesses might work better with specific types of content. A tax preparation firm might do best with blog posts explaining changes in tax laws, for instance. A baseball training facility could benefit from having video posts showing people learning how to play the game or honing their skills. Your work has to be organized correctly, and you have a smart plan in mind.

7. Be careful when getting them ready.

Don't run too many social media campaigns. Know how well you can handle individual ones without getting overwhelmed. While you can work with as many social media sites as you want, only commit to what you are comfortable with handling at any given time. You do not want to forget about individual sites.

You can always use the analytical features from many social media sites to see what is happening with your pages. Analytics examines how many visitors reach your site or interact with your posts. You can use analytics to assess the progress of paid campaigns you operate. This research will help you determine whether to stay with a particular platform or if you are better off elsewhere. Do not use anything too complicated or hard to follow because after all, your workload will get more difficult.

If needed, there is also the option to network with others in your business to work with different campaigns. You could hire one person to run a Facebook campaign while another works on LinkedIn, for instance. See how well those people handle individual campaigns and if they understand how certain social media platforms work. Allow multiple people to work with several channels at a time if you have to, but see that they understand what they are working with. The key is to keep everything in your social media campaign consistent and under control.

Remember that all the points introduced in this chapter are mere suggestions. You could always work with any of the social media sites you are reading about in this guide. Consider what each of these sites has to offer so you can do more with your work.

This book includes details on all the individual sites for online marketing. Look at these points to get ideas on what works best for your social media needs. Discover how to use these places and understand the types of audiences that you could contact, also the positive aspects and pitfalls of a website.

Chapter 4 – An Introduction to Facebook

Let's start by looking into individual platforms. To begin, we need to regard the place that practically started the revolution.

The first social media platform to consider is Facebook. To say that Facebook has made a direct impact on society and the online world would be an understatement.

When Mark Zuckerberg started Facebook while at Harvard, he did it with the intention of simply getting people to communicate with each other at school. Facebook has done more than that. It has grown into a social media platform where anyone with a voice can share things with other people online.

Zuckerberg started the site in 2004 and made it available to colleges all around the world. In 2006, the site opened up to allow anyone 13 years of age or older to register an account.

Since then, the number of people around the world on Facebook has blossomed. It is estimated that as of the middle part of 2017, around 2.1 billion people around the world are on Facebook. There are nearly a billion active users too; this refers to the people who have logged onto Facebook within the past month.

A vast majority of countries around the world use Facebook too. In fact, Facebook has become such a global phenomenon that the United States isn't even the most popular country in the world in terms of Facebook users. While Facebook has around 240 million accounts in the United States, there are around 245 million accounts in India. The platform has also grown in Brazil, the United Kingdom, Thailand, and Canada and many other parts of the world.

Key Points About Facebook

To see why Facebook is a popular place to promote your work, you need to understand what makes it so valuable to people around the world. Many of these points are ones you should explore with regards to your marketing. These will directly influence what you can do with Facebook.

Connect with Friends

With Facebook, people can easily communicate with their friends. People can produce their own 'friends list' on the site. This lets people get in touch with others right away or to be able to see what those people are posting online.

This is vital for businesses. Businesses that market themselves on Facebook could be added by individuals as friends. This lets those users see everything you are posting. They will be reminded of all the things you are doing online. They will continue to recall your name, what you offer, when you are active and produce regular messages.

With this in mind, you will get more long-term customers once they become friends on your site. Those friends will support you and read all about the things you want to do over a long period of time. You will build brand loyalty after a while, as those friends will follow all your posts.

Photo Support

Facebook was one of the first social media sites for people to add photos online. While some other social media sites have incorporated photos quite well, Facebook was an early adopter of this. The service introduced support for photos to help people express themselves in a unique manner.

This is useful for your marketing plans as you can use the photo support feature from Facebook to promote new products or services in a more detailed way. You could illustrate to your viewers what a new product looks like. It could include a picture of something or even a detailed listing of what it offers. Sometimes a photo can say more than just words.

It should be noted that Facebook does have a partnership with Instagram. This link between the two platforms means many people can get their Instagram posts linked to Facebook accounts. Details on this will be introduced later in this guide.

Comment Support

Every post you put on Facebook can be commented upon. That is, a person could respond to any message you post online. Comments are added to help people interact with one another. People could ask you questions about what yourpost. You could then add your responses.

This is all about facilitating a great conversation with others. More importantly, it produces that human side you need to add in your marketing campaign.

Facebook is one of the most important social media sites in the world. This site has revolutionized the way people interact with each other. It is no surprise that so many people are interested in marketing their businesses on Facebook. Large corporations use Facebook all the time to talk with their customers and to take action for whatever is going on in the world right now. They do this to show that they understand what people want and what they are thinking about. You can do the same with a series of carefully orchestrated posts and images.

Like with anything else, be cautious about how you leave comments and remarks. Never add comments that might be harsh or rough. There might also be times when people abuse

Facebook and become hostile to others through the site. Watch what you say as people are going to listen and take note. There is a chance that someone could take a screenshot of an unfortunate post before you delete it trying to cover your tracks.

Analytics Helps

Facebook offers a full analytics feature to check how well your site is running. This includes complete information on who is visiting your site and how they are interacting with individual posts. This helps identifying what is working correctly and what needs to be fixed. It also includes a look at the reach of your campaign, how often people click on certain things on your site and so forth. You could even learn about the specific demographics relating to those who come onto your site.

Read the section later in this guide on how analytics works for Facebook and what you can get out of it. You will get more out of your site when you review your analytics.

Available for Mobile Use

One of the best parts of Facebook is that it adapts to desktop and mobile devices. The amazing thing about Facebook is that it uses its own app that reads everything you would see on your computer but on a smaller tablet or Smartphone screen. This makes it easy for people to read things on your Facebook page even if away from their larger computers. The Facebook app for Android and iOS devices is one of the most popular apps in the world; some phone models even come with the app pre-installed.

Facebook uses a setup for the mobile app that converts the content that you read on your browser and moves it into a smaller and more compact layout that can be read on a mobile device. This is a convenient and useful layout that ensures the content being posted is not unusual in its appearance. Best of all, a phone does not have to struggle to load a full desktop site. You could always use the app yourself to post messages or to respond to people. Regular push updates from the app could also remind you when people are interacting with your Facebook page even when you are on the go.

The mobile support that Facebook offers is very important. You will have to market yourself on Facebook to reach a larger audience that might be looking for information on your business via their phones. Getting onto mobile devices also ensures you will reach a larger audience because some people might be more interested in going online to find you on a mobile device.

A Diverse Layout

Facebook is very popular by one of the most diverse groupings of people you can find on any social media site. With Facebook, you can contact various people regardless of age, gender, race, or education. People of all types reach out to Facebook all the time to talk with each other and share things. They love how Facebook offers a dynamic layout where people can do whatever they want when interacting with each other.

In fact, it is estimated that nearly two-thirds of the entire adult population in the United States use Facebook. That number has grown exponentially in recent years as more businesses and groups have been working with the site. It is interesting to see how Facebook has become the crossroads of the world. Facebook is also a site that so many businesses from every corner of the world choose to advertise. They know that the audience is there.

Problems With Facebook

While it is true that you can get some great things out of your Facebook page, you will have to be aware of a few problems relating to the social media system. These are legitimate concerns but do not have to be a burden if you know how to use Facebook correctly.

Easy to Share Too Much Information

The problem with Facebook is that the site offers you the ability to share a little more information than what you might want to give. You should still try and get as much information on your work out there as possible, but that does not mean that you have to share things that are sensitive or personal. If anything, being a little secretive might help stir the reader's imagination, thus making that person even more interested in what you offer. The key is to use your judgment to decide what information you want to share. This helps designing a great layout without being hard for anyone to follow.

Think carefully when posting anything on Facebook. Think about how you will share things while also considering what appears on other peoples' feeds. Not everything you post is private. Besides, sometimes a bad message could be captured by a user before it is deleted.

Watch for Fakes

Many people create fake profiles on Facebook. They do this as a means of impersonating other people. This is clearly illegal but, at the same time, it is a tough thing for you to discern. As a Facebook user, your name is reserved. . This is to keep you from the risk of having your identity stolen. Watch out for any profiles that visit and like your page. There might be times when problems arise with other people pretending to like your work.

Easy to Get Lost

Although Facebook is a thrilling place in its own right, the massive audience that Facebook reaches often makes it a challenge for you to get online and focus. The biggest issue with Facebook is that it is easy to keep your voice from being heard. Facebook often displays a large number of trends and topics that circulate.

Facebook is a very important social media platform to use when marketing your business. Before you get Facebook to work for you, it is vital to learn how to get your own page set up. To create a useful Facebook page you need to construct a personal profile as well. The next chapter delves into what you have to do to make Facebook work to your advantage.

Chapter 5 – Setting Up a Facebook Page

The first thing to get Facebook work for your marketing needs is to create your own Facebook page. This page will be designed to market your work and let you interact with others.

Your page is the one thing that people are likely to see when they notice you on Facebook. This is where people will see what you want to share and what makes your work special and attractive. You can use this part of your social media outreach to let people know what you are doing. Whether it entails talking about big events in your workplace or about new developments or products and services, you can use Facebook to talk about whatever you wish to discuss.

Your page will let people see what you are doing in real time. You can mention the developments in your business. You could answer questions relating to the products you offer. It even has the option to describe exclusive details about innovations in your business directly through your Facebook page. Anything you can do to make your work distinct and unique is always appreciated on Facebook. You will be thrilled how well Facebook can work for you.

A page is different from a profile in that you can attract many followers onto a page. You can use the page to post information on what you market and to highlight your wares to other people.

This chapter is about understanding how to get a Facebook page up and running. Such a page can be easy to support if you understand what you want to get out of it and how to produce the best possible content.

Different From a Profile

A page is clearly different from a profile on Facebook. You need a page if you want to market your work to others on Facebook. What makes a Facebook page different from a profile? Why create a page as well as a profile for your marketing purposes?

A profile is not something that works with social media marketing in mind. A Facebook profile is something that you could create for your own personal use. When you sign up with Facebook, you get a personal profile to interact with family members and friends on a more private level.

A Facebook page is different. This focuses on marketing a company or other business endeavors. This allows you to post information about your business while inviting people to 'like' your page and follow it. You will still be able to use the same messaging features and interactive points that Facebook profiles use, but it will all be on a grander scale. You will have no limits to how many people can like your page. This becomes easier to use when marketing things to other people.

A Facebook page gives you the use of analytical features. Analytics can be used to show what you posted at any given time. The statistics will provide you with information to help you review everything on your site based on how people reach it, where people go on the page and so forth. Details on Facebook analytics will be covered later in this guide.

Setting Up a Facebook Profile

You need a Facebook profile created before you build a Facebook page. Every page needs an associating profile. This allows a Facebook user to have access to the page. There are a few steps to get your Facebook profile set correctly:

1. Go to the Facebook home page and click on the Sign-Up box.

2. Enter details: your name, email, birth date and gender.

The birth date is required to confirm that you are old enough to have a profile. The date might also determine the types of content you see on the site. The gender information may establish the demographics, although it could influence some of the things you get on a page.

3. Enter your password information.

The password will give you access to your profile and allows you to edit the page you will create.

4. Check your confirmation email.

Facebook will send an email to the address you have entered. This will confirm that you are signing up for a profile.

5. Click on the link to your email address.

At this point, you will have full access to your profile and hereby confirmed it.

6. Complete as much profile info as possible.

It is easier for your page to be confirmed and established with a detailed profile. Facebook prefers that all profiles of people who run their own pages have enough information about themselves as possible. This information will especially work if you plan to convert your profile into a page, a point that will be covered later in this guide.

The information added to your profile can include anything. It might consist of details about schools you attended, your employer, where you live, and the names of relatives if you wish. It is especially important to include your current location to find you; it is even better when the address is the same as your business.

Don't forget to add a profile photo. Facebook strongly recommends to add a profile photo to identify you. For the best results, upload a recent photo of yourself. Make sure the picture is appropriate and relevant; do not add anything dubious to your profile page.

7. Add a mobile phone number to your profile.

The profile needs a mobile number to confirm your information. This also confirms your identity. You are not required to enter a mobile phone number to use your profile, but it is recommended so it is easier for you to reach your account as needed.

Preparing this profile is important to your success. Plan it carefully to simplify the making of your page. Remember that you can produce as many pages as you want but you can only get one profile.

Creating Your Page

Now with a Facebook profile, you can set up your page. The following process for starting a Facebook page is uncomplicated.

1. Log in to your Facebook profile.

You must have a Facebook profile at the start before you get anything working. Refer to the prior instructions to establish a profile.

2. Go to www.facebook.com/pages/create

3. Choose the type of business that your page is for.

There are multiple options. You can use the basic Local Business option or a Company or Organization if you have something larger to work with. You can even create a separate page for a specific product or brand.

4. Enter the identifying information depending on the type of page you have chosen.

Add details of your business' address, the name of a product or just the business name. The input will vary based on the type of business you are promoting.

5. Click the Get Started button once everything is complete.

You should now have a suitable Facebook page. This is needed to reach more people and to interact with them.

Produce Identifying Information

Add the appropriate identifying information onto your site. This data distinguishes your website from everything else on Facebook. It may also work for search engine requirements, as the data you provided is included in Facebook's integrated search engine, among others. You can always use various keywords in your information section too. These should make your page more visible.

Use the following steps to notate the identifying details of your Facebook page:

1. Name your page.

Enter a name for the page that people will use to find your work. The name could be the same name as your business if desired. Be detailed about your work but make sure to incorporate keywords relating to your business.

2. Add a blurb relating to your page.

The blurb should explain the visitor what your site is about. Tell the audience what your business does. Add keywords to the blurb that are related to your business.

3. Incorporate the contact information on your page.

The contact information must include details of your business, your phone number, and your business address. These are vital to show that your business is legitimate. This information will also help to get people to find you while searching. Like with any other search engine many searches on Facebook are geographically oriented. For example, a person using Facebook in the Toledo area will get access to pages that are based on the Toledo area before anything else in the search results.

4. Add details in the 'About' section.

The About section of your page will include information on everything you have to offer. It can include the following:

- Contact information as listed above.

- Information on what your business does.

- Principles of your business.

- Any milestones or other historical bits of data relating to your business you wish to share.

- Honors or awards your business might have earned.

- Any other forms of recognition; this includes articles about your business in a local newspaper.

- Any keywords or layouts you want to list on your page; these include keywords that you want Facebook to recognize to categorize your site.

The About section should be as detailed as possible. This will let people know everything about what you are doing. You have to be specific so people will know what you are trying to convey. People will want to realize that what you are offering is useful and valuable for their needs.

Using a Good Page Name

It is imperative to create a quality page name. One that reflects what your business is about and illustrates to people what you want to share with them.

The page name must be something about your business. It should illustrate to people what you are selling and information you want to communicate.

You have to be specific. You cannot just state what you are selling and where you are located. You must list your name so people can specifically see who you are. You can always add information about your location and other details elsewhere on your page.

There are a few steps to follow to create your page name correctly:

1. Go to the About section of your page. This is on the left side of the screen.

2. Click the Edit button next to your page name.

3. Enter a new name.

4. Confirm the change after you review the overall request.

This is simple and easy to follow. A new name will be posted at the very top of your site. This new name will be among the first things that people will see on your page. It lets everyone know who you are. When people see what is on your Facebook page, they will associate your work with that name. This establishes a good brand people will learn to trust or recognize.

That name of your page can be used with a special URL that matches up with the name. The new URL may be easier for people to remember or at least present a professional appearance to your site. You need to get enough likes on your page to make it work. This will be discussed a little later on.

What If You Can't Change Your Page Name?

There might be times when you are unable to change your page name. This might be due to the option is not available in your location. More importantly, you might not have a page role that allows you to edit the name.

The page role refers to the position you have for managing a page. This will be useful if you have several people in your business that work on a page. The main administrator would be able to operate the entire page while a few others could work by simply adding posts. The admin would clearly have the most power. Additional details on the Page Roles used in a site will be covered later.

Planning Your Categories

You can get your Facebook page added to a series of categories. People can click these sections to find pages that are relevant to certain interests. This is critical for social media marketing as it helps you market yourself on pages that are relevant to whatever you are promoting.

For example, a professional baseball team might use categories such as Sports and Recreation, Baseball, or Professional Sports to distinguish it from other pages. When a person searches "professional sports," the baseball team will appear on the search results. This allows the team to become more visible.

You can use a couple of categories on your page to make it stand out in certain sections of Facebook. Here are some steps to use for producing the right categories:

1. Go to the About section on your page.

2. Go to the General area and then click the Edit button next to the Category menu.

3. Enter a few categories.

You can choose up to three categories on your site. Facebook has a few drop-down lists that will appear based on the categories you are interested in. Type in what you want to use to promote your work and Facebook will produce lists that offer specific spots for your site to appear.

4. Click the Save button.

You can change your categories later on if needed. Always work with categories that are relevant to your business. You can pick the closest selection that works for your site, provided the data you enter is relevant. Using the right categories makes it easier for people to find your page on a Facebook search.

Adding Things to Your About Page

You have to be careful when adding information on your About page. These details help you itemizing the highlights of your business and what makes it valuable. But to make this all work, examine how well you can add sections to your About page.

Do the following when getting new sections inserted in your About page:

1. Go to the Settings menu at the top of the page.

2. Click on the Edit Page section.

3. Go to the Add a Tab section on the bottom part of the menu.

4. Review the individual tabs available. Click on the Add Tab bar to get any of these sections presented on your About page.

The sections you can use include many options like:

- Hours of operation

- The specific services you are offering

- Details on types of products you want to sell

- Physical address information

- Details of managers or other individuals involved with your business

Try to add as many bits of info as you can. A profile with more of these features filled out will be easier for people to trust in your business. People will notice more about your work and get specifics on what you do. More importantly, people will see that you are serious about getting in touch with them. Add all of these details to make your page profile outstanding.

Impressum Features

An impressum is a legal feature that focuses on the basic concepts and terms of your business. It is not required in all countries but some places, particularly ones in Europe, require businesses to post impressums on their websites. This is also the case with Facebook. You can add an impressum to your Facebook page as a means of explaining that you own your current web presence. This also shows that you are the legal owner of the business that you are trying to promote online.

The following steps are needed to help you get your impressum added:

1. Click on the About section of your page.

2. Click on the Edit Page Info section.

3. Look for the impressum section.

4. Add the relevant information needed for the section.

5. Save the changes when you are finished entering the information into your page.

The rules for what you should add in your impressum will vary based on your industry and where you are located. Check on the legal rules involved with getting your impressum added onto a site before you work on it. It does help to add as much information as possible just to be safe, but look for information on everything that will work within this critical legal document. This is a very important legal notice to add to your site depending on your location.

Working With Check-Ins

You can use check-ins as a special way of interacting with people. This is important if you have a physical location. A check-in setup encourages people to come to your business and to lets people know that you are at your location. This in turn lets others on Facebook know about your business.

To understand why a check-in is important, it helps to understand what makes it work. A person who wants to visit your physical business site can go to your page and check in when they arrive. This is perfect for marketing as you can add a promotion where a person could get a special reward or a special deal for checking in on Facebook with your location. You should use this option if you want to market something that requires people to visit your physical shop to see it.

You can quickly turn on the check-in button on your site by using the following steps:

1. Go to the About section of your page.

2. Go to the Edit Page Info section.

3. At the Address section, check the box that says you have a street address.

4. Enter the street address that your business is located. This is regardless of whether it is the same as what you entered early on in when drafting your profile.

5. Click the box stating that customers will be able to get to your business through the street address you have listed.

6. Save the changes on your page.

There might be cases where you do not see the check-in option on your About page. You might have to change the categories that your page uses to make the check-in section available. The rules for getting this to work will vary.

It might be best to add a check-in feature even if you don't have a physical shop where people can visit you. You can use a check-in option to activate a location feature for any photos you post online. These include photos that you add to Instagram. The Instagram section of this guide will list additional information on how to use a Facebook location when you're promoting yourself using a photo.

Adding a Call-to-Action Button

You can create a call-to-action on your site but you can also go one-step further by introducing a few buttons relating to that call-to-action. A special button could encourage people to do something. You can program the button on your page to get people to book a service with you, to order something or to have you contact that person by phone or by email.

This part of marketing is great as it gives you the opportunity to promote whatever you offer. It is a convenient and useful feature that gives your visitors a direct invitation to see what you provide.

This also makes it easier for people to take action. A user doesn't have to enter or search for your URL. That person can just click the button. They will be taken immediately to the spot where you want that person to go. This could increase your conversion rate thanks to how simple it is for people to respond to a request.

There are a few steps needed to get a call-to-action buttons added to your site:

1. Go to the Add a Button section near your cover photo. This should appear on a drop-down menu near that photo.

2. Choose any particular button you want to add. This could include any kind of layout that suits whatever you are offering.

3. Enter the information relating to your button.

The button will include the message and provide the reader with a link. The terms vary based on the type of button you choose. Make sure you opt for one that agrees with your site and your business.

4. Select the Test Button option after your button is implemented. This lets you verify if the button works and if it is linking to the site you intended.

The call-to-action button is vital to get people to take action right away. People are more likely to take action if they are being encouraged when they read something unique. You have to let people know what you are doing and get them to respond to you as soon as possible, no matter what you offer.

Get Verified

It is critical to have your Facebook page verified. A verified page is easier to trust. A verified Facebook page will have a check badge at the top. This will confirm that a legitimate person who is associated with the subject matter on that page is running it.

Verification is important as it ensures people that whatever is shared is legitimate and sensible. People might be suspicious of certain sites if they cannot see that they are run legitimately. With verification, you show that your site is trustworthy and useful. You are displaying full control over what you are doing with your Facebook page.

There are two types of check badges that can be found on a Facebook page:

1. A blue check badge says that Facebook can confirm a page of a particular public figure or brand is authentic.

2. A gray check badge states that Facebook has confirmed a page for a business or other organization is authentic.

Your business will more than likely have a gray check badge. This is due to the professional nature of your site.

People trust verified pages more than others. They will support those pages because they know the information on those pages is accurate, detailed, and honest. They will see that a page is also active and regularly posts information.

Verification is not required when marketing your business on Facebook. When you consider how people trust verified pages more than others, it is best that you aim to get the page verified anyway.

Steps for Getting Verified

There are a few steps to get verified. You will need to get a phone ready:

1. Get a profile picture and cover photo applied to your site.

2. Go to the Settings section at the top of your page.

3. Go to the Page Verification section of the General menu.

4. Click on the Verify This Page link.

5. Enter a phone number for your business. The number should be publicly listed.

6. Click the Call Me Now option.

At this point, Facebook should call the number that you sent. It will give you an automated message. It only takes a few minutes for the message to be sent.

7. Enter the verification code in the box on your screen.

The code should be four digits long.

8. After the code is entered, a gray check badge will be visible in a few days.

Facebook will spend some time looking up your information based on the code you have entered. It will analyze your data and then provide you with a check badge. Facebook does this to ensure a legitimate entity is asking for verification not robots or other automated programs.

Getting Verified with a Document

You also have the option to be verified with a document listed in your business' name. You can do this if you don't have a phone number for verification. You can also do this if you have a phone number but you would rather not use it for privacy-related reasons. The verification process requires a few additional steps:

1. Scan the business document and save the image to your computer.

The business document must include a full listing of your business name and address. Try and get as much contact information on the document as possible. See if you can get the logo or other identifying marks for your business included. Make sure the document has an official appearance.

You can use an appropriate letterhead your business uses or even a utility bill to your name. The content must match up with what you have entered on Facebook.

2. Go to the same Verify This Page link on the General Settings section. Look for the option that lets you upload a document.

3. Add the document from the proper spot on your computer and upload it.

4. Give Facebook a few days to review the document for verification purposes. It should take about the same amount of time as if by phone.

You could use a document if you have a business plan ready but do not have a phone or you want to keep your phone data under control. Make sure any documents you send out for verification purposes are clear and easy to read. Facebook needs to match everything you submit with the content on your profile. Be patient as it can take a bit of time for Facebook to review your documents like when it is analyzing your phone data.

Staying Verified

While it is easy to get your Facebook page verified, likewise that it becomes unverified. This happens if you start sharing false information or if you are hurtful to others.

People who feel that your page is harmful to Facebook can report it to administrators to have its verification removed. This would quickly cause your site to be harder to spot, let alone tough to trust.

Proper conduct should be observed while on Facebook so you will not be at risk. There are a few things to do to keep you verified:

- Make sure you keep the information on your site accurate and detailed.

- Do not become hostile or harsh to visitors.

- Be willing to talk with others about things that relate to your business. You can answer any question a guest has.

- Keep your content unique. Facebook could punish sites that try too hard to be like others to the point where they appear to copy information.

Be active and illustrate a vested interest in your site. Although the odds of you getting that verification removed from your page if you are inactive are minimal, you should still think about how well you are marketing yourself online and that you are active when trying to promote your work. That special badge on your site is all about giving people a reason to trust you.

Acquiring a Special URL

One of the biggest problems with first getting onto Facebook is that you will not have a distinct URL. A URL with a bunch of random characters on it might not look very attractive. However, you will get a customized URL after some time. A more established page will have a special URL to give it a more professional look. Even more importantly, it will be easier for a page to be found just by typing in facebook.com and then whatever the name of the business is.

Let's say that you have a business called Jeff's Corner Café. At the start, your URL might read: www.facebook.com/pages/jeffs-corner-cafe/564796847968ref

That does not sound like the easiest URL to have. There's a reason why Facebook does this. Facebook only gives special vanity URLs to businesses that have at least 25 likes. You will be able to acquire your own special URL when you have received enough likes. Facebook does this to ensure that only businesses that are legitimate and active will actually get the URLs they want. (Additional information on how to get likes will be covered later in this guide.)

When Jeff's Corner Café gets 25 or more likes, it can apply for the following URL: www.facebook.com/JeffsCornerCafe

This would be much easier for a person to discover. It is also easier to market a site like this when it comes with a simple URL.

Your special URL cannot be changed after you make it. Make sure the name you have chosen is one that you will stay and be comfortable with for a while.

The best tip is to use a URL that is identical to the name of your business. This makes it easier for people to just type in the name of the business into the URL. People will quickly find your site and get in touch with it. This is perfect for those who know the name of your business but have never been to your Facebook page and want to see it.

Now that you know about getting a special URL, you must use the proper steps to get it. Here are the instructions to use when getting the special URL ready for your site. Remember to apply for this after you have at least 25 likes on your Facebook page:

1. Log into your Facebook account.

2. Go to facebook.com/username.

3. Go to the Select a Username option.

4. Choose the specific page where you want your new username added.

5. Enter the URL name you want to use.

6. Click on the box to check if it is available.

7. Review the terms of use if the URL of interest is available. Click to confirm that you want to use that URL or cancel if you want to choose something else.

Try to get as many URL options as possible. This is so you have some backup options in the event that you have problems getting one URL ready. Review how well the process for producing a page is organized and that you have a good plan for getting the most from your work. Get the URL as close to your business name as possible.

Tips for Use

Produce a good URL for your Facebook page. The URL will be important for search purposes as a Facebook search often looks through the URL keywords first. With that in mind, here are a few tips when producing your URL. Remember, you cannot change your URL once you fully create it:

- Try to use a name that you own the rights to. This prevents others from stealing that name.

- Keep the name as close to your actual business name as possible.

- Keywords relating to your business could be added if desired. When you do this, watch for how the keywords match up with what you are marketing. Do not use anything overly verbose or else it could be tough to enter the URL.

- Think about whether or not you plan to get your business name changed. You might need to get another URL reserved later on just to be safe. You would get different Facebook profiles ready for each of the names that you want to use in the future.

After you get your new URL ready, you can share it with others and use it for all your marketing. This is a convenient feature of Facebook, which lets you market your work to a larger audience. You will see that it is easy to get people to see your site when you use a URL.

Converting a Facebook Profile to a Page

Perhaps you are trying to get your Facebook profile promoted a little more in your marketing campaign. The problem is there is a limit to how many people can follow a profile. You can only have 5,000 people follow your profile. Nevertheless, you can get an existing Facebook profile converted into a new page. This is ideal if you have a large amount of data or content on your profile and you want to use it for marketing purposes.

As you convert your Facebook profile into a page, the data on that profile moves to a new spot. This is where you have full control over for your marketing. Your profile information and photo will be carried to that new page. You can still edit the information on the page, as you like to. You can even access some tools to help you handle your information up to 14 days after the conversion process is complete.

You will still be able to adjust the page from your personal profile account. This is vital to the process of editing your work, as it will be simplified. The page will also be fully functional on both mobile and desktop devices. This makes it easier for you to get your content seen by more people. It is very important if you want to get more out of a page without it being too hard to follow or use.

Do you have a Facebook profile that you want to convert to a page? You can get a Facebook profile produced on its own specific page. The following steps will help you getting anything you already have filled out and organized.

1. Make sure you are logged in to the profile that you want to convert into a page.

2. Go to the migrate option on Facebook to get the process started. This is available at www.facebook.com/pages/create/migrate.

3. Click on the Get Started button.

4. Look at the information that has been uploaded to your page. Make sure the data is reviewed and change anything that needs changing.

At this point, the site should be fully functional and ready to use. Facebook has also produced various sections on the page that will help you with arranging everything you use. Using this properly will get it all taken care of quickly. This way you will have complete access to the content you want to work with.

Make sure the profile you are converting is relevant to your business. You cannot afford to let your social media marketing efforts become personal. The profile has to be directly about the business and informative to readers. Anything that is too personal could become unappealing and could even feature words or values that conflict with what you want your business to express to others.

Chapter 6 – Establishing the Best Facebook Posts

One massive part of running your own Facebook site is creating posts that are sensible and easy to read. The posts you produce must be detailed and include information that relates to your business. This chapter is about understanding what you should do when creating an ideal series of Facebook posts for your marketing. You will be impressed how well it succeeds if you think about how to make it work right.

Part of creating Facebook posts entails getting messages that not only draw the visitor's attention but also make people want to forward your messages. As your posts are forwarded to others, it becomes easier to market your work.

Tell Stories

Some of the best posts to add on your Facebook page are stories. Talk about anything you want on your Facebook page as long as they are relevant and unique. Tell stories that relate to your business and let people know what makes what is special. The best stories are forwarded to others.

Be willing to talk about your business' background. Share what you have been doing and why you are so motivated to help them. Show that what you are doing is making a difference in the lives of others; people will support you if they see itis worthwhile and useful.

You could tell stories about how people use your services. A photo or video depicting what someone is doing with your products could be worthwhile. This works best if you have a more established business. This also works if you want to display some new product or service your business offers.

Work With Trending Topics

The Facebook search algorithm rewards people who talk about trending issues. A popular topic will be highlighted more often as it is something people are more likely to search for or has a strong demand to discover. Working with trending topics that are specific and important is always useful.

By discussing trending topics, it becomes easier for you to be noticed. You will show that your business understands the trends and interests of today. This gives you the opportunity to share data with others in a distinctive way.

Be careful how you incorporate these trends into your work. Do not talk about something that has nothing to do with your business just because that topic is popular. Try to relate the trend to your business in some way. This is always worth promoting.

Talk About Business Decisions

People appreciate transparency and it is an important part of running a business. Potential customers prefer businesses that are open and direct about what they want to do or promote. Customers appreciate those entities that are willing to talk about what inspires them and the reasons why they are in business.

You can converse about any business decision and how you operate with others. Talking about results and ideas makes you more open to the readers. You can even ask for feedback about anything you want to follow up on. As you get a clear idea of what people want, getting information from your fans can make a difference.

Whatever the case might be, always be open to your followers. Let them know as much as you can tell them about what you are doing. It will noticed that people who understand back what you offer. That in turn promotes a sense of trust and support from your readers.

Use Unique Media

Although anyone can post historic images, pictures from the news or even memes on their Facebook feeds, it is always best to be unique and personal. Part of this involves using media files and images that are specific and unlike everything else. These files people can study and say that they got it from you and no one else.

When you use unique media files, you show your viewers that you have a great plan in mind for your business. They realize you are creative and inventive while always having an open mind. Using the same type of image that everyone utilizes is not always best as it just shows repetition.

You have no limits as to what you can use in your media. You can take photos of your workplace or images of any products. You could even offer images of prototypes of something to sell later on. Anything that supports your content is always great to incorporate.

Can You Offer Exclusive Deals?

Some businesses like to use Facebook to promote special discounts and rebates that are only available to people who go to the Facebook page. These include promo codes to use on a website or details on how to get an exclusive in-store discount. Although these are great offers, they are not essential. You can add them if you want, but the goal is not to just offer discounts but rather to make people notice what you have.

Discounts can make your business stand out, but it is even more important to tell people about your business based on what you have to offer. The discounts you add are just a small part of what you put forward.

Discounts are used as ice-breakers to get people to think about what you offer. But when you post information on special deals, add other posts afterwards about what makes your business or its products or services worthwhile. Let people know that what you are offering is trustworthy and is important to their lives.

Highlight Items in Use

Are you trying to promote certain products or services by showing people how they function? Use Facebook to do that. Post a short video of something you are offering in action. Add a few photos displaying what your products do and how they work. Be clear and specific in your videos so it is clear and there is no chance of misunderstanding or being confused.

Four Key Steps for Posting

Regardless of what you plan on posting, think about what you have to do to get your message out there. There are four important steps to get a post ready:

1. Consider the purpose of your post.

Think about why you want to post a message about in the first place. Consider the end game of your post and why you feel that message is important. Having a good plan is critical to controlling the messages. Each post should have some kind of meaning about your products or services. You should avoid sharing anything that could be confusing or misleading or does not directly relate to what your business is.

You might have a post that will introduce people to a new product or service. Maybe you want to express the virtues of your business, so people will be more interested in what you offer. Whatever the case, you must produce a post that is inviting, has information, and is intriguing.

2. Review how personal your message is.

A message can be personal and include details on what you or other people are doing in a business. You might even talk about the influences relating to your work, why you are doing something and why you are promoting a particular product or service. You could even give people a history of your business about what inspired you to start working in a particular field. Being personal about your work is always worthwhile, but first you should examine how well the message is being orchestrated. Do not add many personal details unless you feel that they are relevant to your work and will not compromise anything. Avoid creating messages that are overly simplified.

3. Think about the promotional aspect of the message.

A message should have a promotional feature that explains to the viewer what you wish to discuss and why what you share is important. The promotional angle you produce should be based on what you feel. It is vital to your message.

Make your messages intriguing to your potential viewers. They should invite people to see what you have to offer. Don't be overly needy. Make your messages appealing while still convincing the readers that what you have is worthwhile.

4. Make sure your message is relevant to your company culture.

Your message should be based on the company culture you want to express. Only create messages that are relevant to your company's culture and are illustrative of what you want to express to the audience. Be careful of how you say things and that you are not departing from what you represent.

Your Facebook page needs to have an appearance in line with your goals. The personality should be consistent as it shows you are serious about promoting yourself. You have to express that you want to help your readers and that you have something of value they will be interested in using.

This does not mean you cannot have a bit of personality. A friendly touch to your work and plenty of interaction and fun is always worthwhile. Don't write about something that is extreme; it might confuse your audience.

The proceeding four aspects of creating a post will give you a better idea of what to express to your audience members. Plan your posts on Facebook based on these features and you will make your ads attractive and valuable.

How Long Should a Post Be?

There are no real rules on Facebook as to how long a post should be. But since most people don't want to spend all day reading, try and keep your posts as short as possible. Your messages could be around 100 words at the most. Anything with more rich media content like videos or images would especially help to make something more interesting and easier to read.

Do not overdo it when creating something attractive. A long post might be good for a press release or when you want to explain something in detail. Without it being complicated or otherwise hard to follow; make your offer simple enough so it can be distinguished.

Don't Forget Frequency

Keep your posts frequent, but don't go overboard on it either. It is fine to add posts every day or every other day or even on specific days of the week. However, whatever you do, keep some space in between each of your posts. Avoid adding too much all at once or else people will lose track of your content. It is easy for your content to be muddled and hard to follow if you have too many posts all at once. Too many posts all at once can make your site hard to read.

Chapter 7 – Keys For Running a Facebook Page

Now that you understand how to create your own Facebook page and how to add things to it, be aware of how well your page is working. Whatever you use should be organized and simple to follow or utilize. You must use a few trouble-free strategies for getting your Facebook page up and running. These give your site a special layout that is easy to follow and gets everyone in your workplace to have a good plan ready for maintaining the page.

Getting the Roles Ready

When readying your Facebook page, you will probably work with many others at the same time. This includes you and other partners in your business. Your social media marketing plans must be organized properly with everyone in your workplace banding together to get the word out about what you offer.

Each person will have different roles when getting your Facebook page up and running. There are six different roles on a Facebook page. Each of these roles has its own rules for how to keep Facebook working to make it ideal and helpful.

Setting Up Roles

Prepare a number of roles for your individual members to get on Facebook. Here's how to set up individual roles:

1. Go to the Settings section at the top of the page.

2. Go to the Page Roles section on the left-hand column.

3. Enter a name or email into the proper section.

4. Select the person that you want to utilize that particular role.

5. Click the Editor option and choose the role that the person will follow from the list on the menu.

6. Click on the Add button and then enter your password to let Facebook know that person will have a certain role.

This is a simple process, but you should acknowledge what the roles for use are. Select the right people for each of these roles based on their capabilities, their knowledge of Facebook, and how responsible they are with producing valuable content. The roles that are run on a Facebook page are as follows:

Admin

This person has the most duties for a page. The person who runs the business could be the admin although that could be delegated to anyone else in the workplace. The admin, or administrator, does the following:

- Manages roles on the page.

- Adjusts the overall settings of the page.

- Creates and deletes posts.

- Can go live and interact with people through video on a mobile device.

- Responds to or deletes comments from other people.

- Creates ads or promotions.

- Reviews the analytics features.

- Removes and bans people from a page.

The work of the admin is the most important as that individual will have the right to change what happens on the page at any time. It is vital to see that all actions on the site are run by an admin who understands how the site works. This is all about producing a sensible approach for handling content.

Editor

The editor is the second most powerful on a Facebook page. This person actually has almost all the same duties as the admin. However, the editor cannot manage Page Roles or settings. The editor will not necessarily work with the general functions that come with a site. It is vital to watch that this role is delegated properly.

Moderator

The moderator can send messages to other people, respond to, delete comments, and create advertisements. Nevertheless, they cannot create or delete posts or go live. The moderator is simply someone who edits a page and interacts with the people who comment on it. The moderator cannot write anything new outside of the responses left on the site. In other words, the moderator is simply keeping the conversations produced on the page under control to where everything listed is highlighted in a carefully orchestrated manner.

Advertiser

An advertiser is someone who focuses on creating advertisements on Facebook. They are responsible for preparing ads that appear on a page. They can also review the analytics relating to the advertisements posted. This role is vital to determine how well a page is produced and how individual messages are applied. Anyone who understands how to market things to people and can analyze those ads carefully will be worth having as an advertiser. Choose this role carefully.

Analyst

The analyst focuses more on reviewing how a page works. That person has full access to the analytics through Google Insight. The Analyst will see how well the site is working and can figure out ways to have site run better. The person's role is extremely minimal, but at the same time, it entails working to examine how a site can be run. The analysis helps to see how different sections of a site are accessed. It is about optimizing the efforts to reach a greater variety of people.

Live Contributor

The last of the roles is a live contributor position. They will go live on a page as a special live video contributor from a mobile device. They are responsible for promoting your work through a live video feed. Such individual should be charismatic, and their job is to highlight something online to other people. The Live Contributor will not actually contribute to the page outside of the video. They do not even have access to the insights page. You are simply entrusting a person with this role to handle the live interactions with others.

Be careful in choosing the right people to take on the roles on your page. In most cases, you can be the admin although you do have the option to let someone else do that. Just be careful when figuring out what you want to get out of your work. Let ones who understand how to use Facebook to will handle it in a careful manner.

Customizing Your Page

One useful part of marketing yourself on Facebook involves creating a page that is distinct and fully customized. People will be more interested in your work if they see that it has been customized in some way. They will learn more about you and see that you are serious about your marketing. Some might also be interested in your work based on what you have listed. Here are a few recommendations when customizing your Facebook page.

Using a Cover Photo

The cover photo refers to the big landscape bar that appears on the top of your page. This is separate from the profile photo you use. The cover photo should be detailed and have a clear layout while being easy to distinguish. It should be attractive and explain what your business does or has some image relevant to what you are promoting. You can change the photo regularly depending on what you offer or what you want to promote through some special. Make sure that anything you use is relevant and sensible for your marketing plans.

To add a cover photo:

1. Hover over the cover photo and click the Change Cover option on the top-left.

2. Click to upload a photo or video that you want to use from your hard drive.

3. Review the photo and how it will be displayed on the screen. You can resize or edit it in any way you see fit.

4. Click Save to save the photo.

Be certain that the photo you use is relevant to your site and appropriate for use. Look for something that is inviting and gets people interested.

Customize the Tabs

The tabs on the left-hand side of your screen can be adjusted. You can add tabs that reflect things like videos, photos, events coming up and so forth. These tabs will lead people to places where they can learn more about you. They can also find specific bits of content.

To adjust the tabs:

1. Go to the More tab on the Editor.

2. Click on the Manage Tabs option.

3. Drag the tabs to arrange them into different slots.

4. Click the Add or Remove Tabs option to decide which tabs you want to add.

5. You will be on the Facebook Apps menu at this point. Decide which items you want to add to your tabs. This should give you access to a program that lets you add or remove content into that new section.

Add as many tabs as you wish. Only add the ones that you know you will use for a while. You need plenty of content in each of these tabs. These don't have to be updated as often as your main page, but they should still include enough content to highlight whatever you offer. This is essential for the general success of your site.

Add a Ratings or Review Section

One custom feature to add is using a ratings or review section. This is similar to what you would find on specialized review sites. It lists information on what people think about your business. It ranks you out of five stars. The section can also list how many people have reviewed your site in the past. Any place with lots of four or five-star reviews will be unproblematic to trust.

This is only available if you are listed as a local business during the setup process. Also, you have to include your entire physical address to access it.

This process offers a simple way to get your reviews added:

1. Click on the Settings option at the top part of the page.

2. Click on the Edit Page section on the left-hand column.

3. Choose the Add a Tab option.

4. Look for the Reviews section.

5. Switch the Show Reviews section to the On spot.

6. Choose where the Reviews tab will be located among the tabs. You should be able to drag it up or down. You might value reviews more if you put it higher up on the page.

Adding reviews is great as it allows you to receive feedback. People can give you a review, also leave a brief comment about their experience with your business, thus providing a detailed response on how well your work is being utilized and provided. This feedback can help you see peoples opines about your business. This can be helpful to get an idea of what you need to fix. Of course, a place with many great reviews will be more appealing as it shows that you are obviously doing something right.

On a related note, always ask people to leave reviews if they have had good experiences with your products or services. Ask for these reviews if you believe people like what you are doing. They are useful, but watch for how you offer services. Typically, people are likely to leave bad reviews if they are upset about something.

Establish a Strategy

As you plan your Facebook page, you have to work with a good layout that features a smart and useful strategy. Produce a strategy that illustrates useful details to your readers. This lets people see what you have to offer in a useful and appropriately organized manner.

When you arrange your Facebook page, ask a few questions about your strategy:

- Who are you trying to target? Who do you feel is going to read your site?

- Look at how you will position your site. The layout should be organized where people can easily understand what you want to discuss online.

- Decide on an appropriate tone of voice. It should be consistent all the way through. The tone must be fitting to your business and illustrate what you want to say and share.

- Review how your business is different from what someone else is offering. Try to keep the data from being similar to what other people have posted.

Check the Comments Regularly

You will certainly find comments on your Facebook posts. Check regularly for what people are saying. Look at any trends relating and respond to any questions or issues as soon as possible. Be prompt in your responses so people can trust you and what you offer them.

You can position several people to work as moderators who will review comments. Make sure these are reviewed often so you not only keep things civil but also to show a human side to your business. See how others in your business respond to them by giving them roles for accessing your comments and responding to them as required. Create a consistent voice for those responses.

Produce a Schedule

A schedule for running a Facebook page could be repeated on any other social media platform. However, this goes double for Facebook, which is what people are more likely to use it than other sites. You must establish a schedule for posts.

Think about a schedule that you can actually keep but make it is sensible and easy for you to keep. It should be one you can work with and simple to maintain. This is all about giving you more control over how well your schedule is laid out and how you can easily get online and do more.

What Time of Day?

One idea is to post your messages at specific times of the day. You could schedule a post at noon or three in the afternoon each day. Getting regular messages out at a certain time makes it easier for people to trust your site. They will see that you have a plan for getting things out on a regular basis and that you have a strict routine, and you are persistent.

People say that it is best to post something at noon or around three or six in the afternoon. These are times when people might be online. Does this mean it is always a good time to post something? The problem with posting a message during peak hours is that your posts will be competing with many others. A follower's feed could be clogged to the point where your messages are forgotten or discarded.

With this in mind, experiment with timing your posts. Be willing to try different times to check what reaction you receive. Test yourself regularly and see what develops, and the comments, so you can change the timing of your posts accordingly.

What About Country and Age Limits?

Another thing you can do when creating a Facebook page is to build limits as to who can visit the site. This might sound contradictory to efforts to make your site visible to everyone. The truth is that it might contain something that is off limits to a certain audience. For instance, you might be selling a product that cannot be imported to a specific country. You could also be selling something that cannot be sold to people under a certain age in a particular state or nation.

For instance, you might be running a craft brewery. You can fashion a Facebook page that highlights all the stuff that your brewery offers. But you must also have a limitation so that people under the age of 21 or whatever the legal drinking limit is in your country cannot access the page. This not only shows that you are responsible but also that you care about the laws relating to what you offer.

A few steps can be used for helping you to establish these limits on your site:

1. Go to the Settings section at the top of your page.

2. Reach the General section.

3. Go to the Country Restrictions or Age Restrictions section.

4. Enter the details on what restrictions you wish to add.

5. Save the changes.

Adding these limits is vital for legal reasons. This may work for your marketing. It shows that you are responsible and that you understand the legal and ethical concerns regarding something you might be selling. For instance, if you were to sell cigar accessories, it would be a bad idea to give access to your page to people under the age of 18. You might also establish limits where people from countries with extremely strict laws against using cigars or other tobacco products would not have access to your site.

Always use these points when making your Facebook page work for you. It is vital that you keep your page organized and visible so people will be interested in what you are offering and are willing to invest in your business.

Chapter 8 – Working with Facebook Groups

Facebook is great for more than just talking to individuals. You can also set up larger communities with the Facebook Groups feature. This is a special point to participate in a section where you can discuss anything about your business. Organize a group with the intention of promoting a very specific event or a product or service you want to highlight. Or a group that is all about what you offer. You can also join a group and promote yourself through those groups too if you prefer to do that instead of starting a completely new group.

Facebook has organized its groups in many forms. You can find groups devoted to specific products or industries that you are associated with. Get your existing Facebook page or profile exposed to a group or at least get people to hear more about your business site in general. It is rather easy to make your work visible to more people who are interested in your specific group when you use Facebook Groups.

Joining a Group

To start, we should talk about how you can join a group. Find a group related to your line of work and join it so you can talk with other people. As you join a group, you will discuss things related to what you are doing. This lets you interact with people in a special way. You are sharing things with people who are interested. This works best when you join a group that is relevant to whatever your business is or what you are marketing.

Use these basic steps to connect with a group:

1. Look on Facebook to find a group. You might need to use the search engine bar at the top of the site to find a group related to your interests.

2. Click on a link for the group and be sure it is relevant to what you want to discuss.

3. Click on the Join Group link located below the cover photo.

When you join a group, people who like your page might see an update saying that you are joining the group. Make sure it is sensible and appealing not only to you, but also your followers. Don't pick controversial or inappropriate topics that might cause some of your fans questioning what you are doing.

Others will never know that you are joining a group if it is a private one. Even then, you might have to wait to enter a password or to receive acceptance from an admin to join it. Such a group would have limits on who it would allow to join because it has specific standards or it wants to restrict its memberships to only those who actually understand what is being offered on a page.

Be careful with how you converse with people on your site. Make sure you avoid being too promotional when talking with a group. Some groups might ask you to avoid talking about your business or promoting your work. Others might feel that you are being too needy or demanding of others in the group if you talk about your business too much. Be careful how you interact with others so you will not struggle with trying to get a great link up and running.

Creating a Group

You can start your own group on Facebook too. A group would let you market things related to your business or even let people who support your business share information. This is perfect if you have an established base to maintain. By creating a group, you are letting people get in touch with you and hear more about whatever you want to provide them.

The following steps to create your own group:

1. Go to the top-right arrow menu on your Facebook page.

2. Click on the Create Group section. This should be on a drop-down menu after you click on the proper arrow.

3. Enter the details relating to your group:

The details of your group listing should include:

- The name of your group

- The members you want to add

- Privacy settings; this includes details on any passwords you want to use, how old people should be to have access to the group or where they are located.

4. Add a cover photo. This can differ from what you are using on your main page.

5. Add a description that lists points on what your site is about and what you want to offer to potential members.

6. Click on the Create button.

Adding Members

You can always add members to your Facebook group, but a few points should be considered:

1. Start by soliciting memberships into your group. You can post a message on your site listing what people can do to access your site.

2. Go to the page of the group that you want to add your new members.

3. Click on the Add Members section located below the main photo.

4. Enter the details on all the people you want to add to your group.

This takes a bit of effort and time because you examine the individual requests people are sending. It might take a few days to get all your requests handled depending on how many you get. Your visitors will probably understand that it takes a bit of time for them to all be accepted. They will surely wait knowing that the wait will be worth it so long as you produce a quality group.

Removing or Blocking People

Abusive members of your group may hurt your marketing efforts. You do not want to get trolls or other negative people to slander what you do or to disrupt or harass others. Any objectionable person could keep the main goals from working as well as they should. Learn how to remove or block those people.

1. Go to the Members section of your group page.

2. Check for the member or members that you want to remove from your page.

3. Click on the ... section next to a person's name.

4. Click the Remove From Group option.

5. Review the boxes next to that person when removing that person from a page.

There is ane option to remove a person's posts or comments. You can also delete any pending invites that a member has sent out to other people. All of these items can be removed from your page if you have determined that a person in question might be harmful to others.

6. Permanently blocking a person from ever coming back is another solution. You would have to check the Block Permanently option to block someone.

7. Click on the Confirm button after everything is covered.

Blocking unwanted people is important for the safety of your group. It is easier for people to be convinced of negative things about businesses than it is for them to see that a business is actually positive. Always block undesirable people from your group and keep the atmosphere supportive and attractive.

Removing Someone from Your Block List

You can also remove a block from someone if you deem that it is safe to bring that person back to your site. Use these steps to make that work:

1. Go to the Members section of the group page.

2. Click on the Blocked section. This includes details on everything that you have blocked from your page.

3. Click the Remove Block option next to any name.

Be sure to use this only when people can be trusted again. You have the complete discretion as to who should be regaining access to your site. Be careful deciding what you can do to admit people who are not going to spoil your page or return to their old behaviors that resulted in being blocked in the first place. The person in question should be treated as if they were given a probationary period and should to be monitored carefully to ensure they will not create nuisances.

How to Leverage Facebook Groups

Now that you have either created or joined a Facebook group, learn how to use it correctly. You cannot just post an ordinary message on a group page. Be a good leader who will strike up great conversations. Be creative and thoughtful of whatever others want to share. This should give you extra help for producing a fine space for conversations where people will want to get in touch with each other. You can also show your assertiveness by sharing your honest opinions.

Utilize Facebook Groups in a variety of ways. Let's look at a few of them to get this special part of Facebook working to your advantage.

Talk About Current Events

One way to leverage Facebook Groups is to discuss current events. Talk with others about things that are taking place in the industry you are devoted to. The key is to prove that you understand the latest trends in the field you are working with. Use this to let people know about how your business relates to what is happening in the world. It could give you a special way to make your business relevant and intriguing. Don't be polarizing or controversial.

Give People Rewards

You can always send rewards for guests who interact with you. These include prizes like special tips or offers on what you sell, share updates, or even unique stories about your work. Anything that encourages people to keep doing business with you while looking at what is available. This strategy works best with a group you have created yourself. Avoid offering rewards on someone else's group page if you can.

Exclusives for people who are in your group are worthwhile too. You can even use this to attract people to your group by offering exclusive rewards to those who join. You do not have to say specifically what those deals or offers are. At least follow through on what you promise.

Ask Questions

You could ask questions about anything relating to your business. You do not have to talk about your business directly. Ask something that relates to what you are offering, so people will be interested. A good question helps you see opinions of others. It could also help you to gauge your audience to figure out what people might expect from your business. This field research gives you a plan for producing an exciting site that can serve everyone's needs.

Promote Events

Are you looking to highlight any events within your business? If so, then you can use Facebook to highlight any of these special occasions. Let people know about things in a group and meet up or they can visit a website to learn more. Again, this is something to do on a group you have created yourself and not on someone else's.

You could also talk about other events that you did not create but have plans to participate. Maybe you will be at a trade show, convention, parade, community service event or something else in your community. Explain that you are going to be there and mention when it occurs. If possible, talk about your role in that event.

Discuss Events

There is also the option to talk about events you have been promoting. It proceeds an event that took place. Invite people to share feedback about an event or to talk about how much fun they had or what they might have seen somewhere. This lets people get a little closer to you as you highlight what you are doing within your business. You could even encourage people to send photos of what they experienced at a certain event. Anything that illustrates in detail whatever you want to promote or share with others is always perfect to share on your page.

Refer to the check-in section of this guide. You could always use a check-in option that links to the event in question. This lets your users confirm that they arrived and invites them to participate and have fun.

Interact With Team Members

Maybe you have many people in your business with whom that you need to contact. You can create a Facebook group that is all about your employees. This would be a private setup where you only invite employees onto the site. It provides a setting where people can discuss business functions or plans to move forward.

This option for using Facebook Groups is not necessarily made with marketing in mind. If anything, you might want to create a private group separate from the public one you want to start. This private spot would require you to add passwords or to restrict people who have access. Having such a private group gives you the option to confer with your workers and to see what everyone in the business is doing. It creates an organized layout to interact with people. Best of all, it becomes easier for you to market your work to others because you are getting new strategies through the conversations you have with your fellow workers.

Facebook Groups are perfect for getting people to interact with you. Whether you choose to create your own group or to join an existing one, you will have plenty of fun. Check out what you can do with your Facebook group, and you will see just how well it can work for you.

Chapter 9 – Creating Facebook Ads

One of the best ways to use Facebook for your marketing needs is by using special paid ads. While many of the things you can do for social media marketing through Facebook are free, you might need to pay a price to get the word out about your work. Facebook will help you in this case with a paid advertisement solution that will work for you.

Great Facebook ads let you do more with your marketing campaigns. They let you get your messages out to a larger number of people thanks to a convenient layout for you to highlight what you offer directly on their Facebook pages. Some ads can also be used on your page, although this works best when you have promo codes or other special offers to highlight. Best of all, this can be customized in many ways.

Like with many other forms of advertising, you will have to spend money on your Facebook ads. You can always use the system for generating ads in a convenient way that is not too hard to follow or use. Produce great Facebook ads with a good plan for making it all work. Create a usable, sensible, and affordable budget for these ads.

How Are Facebook Ads Laid Out?

To see why it is important to create ads on Facebook, look at how well these ads are produced. Facebook ads are made with dynamic bodies that are elaborate and feature some nice points that illustrate everything you want to promote to others.

A Facebook ad can include a design that appears right in the middle of a person's feed. That is, it will look like a typical post, but it will be a fully paid advertisement for your product or service. It can include an image of whatever you are promoting plus your company's logo or other identifying marks. This helps you to make your business more visible as it will stand out and be attractive. It makes your work more dynamic.

Some ads may also appear on the side of a Facebook page. This is similar to what you might notice on Google, Yahoo, or any other search engine. The advertisement will be smaller, but it will still include all the details you want to convey.

These ads are laid out with a setup based on the keywords one is searching for or the subject matter of a site. Sometimes they might be based on a user's perceived interests according to what that person has liked in the past.

Each ad will include its own link to your site or your Facebook page depending on what you post. The ad lets people get in touch with you and will get them out to your site with one click. You need to get people to look at your ads as soon as possible, so it is vital that you use whatever marketing ploy at your disposal.

Some ads can include 'like' buttons next to them. This allows the reader to give you immediate feedback about your posts. It is a good way of getting your site a few more likes. With a simple layout that is not hard to follow, it delivers something outstanding.

Creating a Facebook Ad Campaign

The first thing to do after getting your Facebook profile set up is to create a smart and useful ad. To make this work, go to the Facebook Ads Manager. This feature has a convenient layout that lets you look at the ads you are producing and helps you organize great campaigns. With the Ads Manager, you can create ads, place them in the right spots, and analyze how well they are doing.

To make it all work, you have to go through the campaign process. When you create ads, it is not necessarily making a solitary message you can post at any time. Rather, you are making campaigns that will feature ads that appear many times on different Facebook feeds and searches. Because every persons Facebook experience is unique, you will have to look at how well a campaign is designed and that you have a good plan up and running to make it all worthwhile.

The Ads Manager program on Facebook will guide you through the entire process. The following are some ideas for getting a campaign ready.

Establish an Objective

When producing a new ad campaign the first thing to do is to create a smart objective. Work with these tips to get your objective ready:

1. Determine the type of awareness goal you have.

You can choose to establish either a brand awareness campaign or a reach campaign. With the brand awareness option, you are letting people know about what you offer and how your business is dynamic and unique. This is recommended for those who are just starting out and want to try something new.

A reach option entails simply trying to get your message out to a larger number of people. It will have a greater coverage level that will work best if you have already created an awareness option.

2. Determine the overall consideration for your efforts.

The consideration for the campaign refers to what specifically you want to get from your work. This could be getting more traffic to your site, getting more video views, having more people download and install any app you have, or to simply generate leads. The campaign you produce will need to be adjusted based on the results you want to get from your leads.

3. Figure out the specific type of conversion you will be working with.

The conversion refers to how you will get people to buy your products or services. You can choose to create conversions in the form of online sales or visits to a physical store. The tasks and features in your campaign will vary based on the conversions you want to work with.

Producing an Ad Set

After you have figured out the goals, decide on the overall ad set you want to use and get it ready. An ad set is a series of ads that meet the objectives you want. You can get as many ad sets produced as you want but they should all meet the overall goals you have for getting more people to visit your site. There are a few things you can do when getting such a set ready:

1. Create a name for your ad set.

Give your set any name you wish. Make sure the name is distinct and that you can tell it from any other campaigns you want to run.

2. Determine your audience.

Decide on the specific audience you want to target within your group. The audience can include one of many groups including the following:

- People within a certain location; you have the option to add as many locations as you want.

- People in a particular age range; these include people as young as 18 or those in the 65 and older group.

- People who speak specific languages; this could work if you are targeting a certain region where many languages are spoken.

- Those of a certain gender; you can choose to target both men and women or just one group.

- Anyone with certain interests; Facebook lets you enter keywords that relate to particular interests.

The worst thing you could ever do when marketing yourself is to be generic. You cannot assume that everyone in the world will be interested in your work. Work toward targeting the audience that will actually be interested in your content. The overall reach might be small, but you will not target the people who probably don't have an interest in your work and only those who will notice.

3. Use the detailed targeting feature for very specific groups.

Detailed targeting allows you to search Facebook to find detailed and exact groups where you could market your wares. This would be choosing to work with people based on extremely particular demographics, their interests, or any opinions they might express while on Facebook.

4. Add the specific connections you want to follow.

People who express certain connections to your site can get access to your ads. You can add connections where people will be more likely to see your ads based on things like the following:

- What pages they have been on

- Whether people have liked your page

- Any interactions someone has made with your page in the past

- Events relating to your business as listed on your page

The connections you choose are important to help you decide what is available.

Determine Where the Ads Will Be Placed

Now that you know what you want to do with your campaign, you will decide the exposure of your advertisements. The following steps will help you to get your ads out to the right spots. These are all to be found on the Placements section of the Ads Manager:

1. Go to the Placements section of your site and list where your work will go.

You can decide where on Facebook or on any other site owned by Facebook your ads will appear on. Make sure you carefully analyze what is available.

2. Review the individual parts of Facebook where you can get your ads placed.

Choose to add your posts onto feeds, instant articles, in-stream videos, or suggested video listings, among others. You could also ask to have your ad appear around a certain keyword. This is provided you decide on the correct keyword(s) for your ads. The Ads Manager system will let you determine which specific feeds or features you want your ad to appear.

Put a decent value on your ad so it will be more likely to show up. Your ad might not even appear if it is too cheap. This point will be discussed after the finances for your marketing campaign is determined.

3. Determine where on Instagram you want to get your ads placed.

Facebook has a sizable share in Instagram, another social media platform that you will read about later in this guide. You can choose to add your advertisements onto Instagram by getting your ads onto a person's particular feed. It is optional to get your Facebook ads listed on Instagram, but this could work when you consider how popular Instagram has become recently.

4. Decide on which devices to have your ads appear.

You can get your ads to appear on all devices, or you can just ask to get your ads to appear on Smartphones and tablets and not on larger desktop or laptop browsers. For the results, it is best to have your ads appear on all devices. You might want to use a mobile-only approach if you are adamant on selling something like a mobile app or if you are targeting people who are visiting a certain location and are far from their regular computers. The Ads Manager section here will let you choose the devices you want your ads placed.

5. Let your ads appear automatically in different places.

Although you could let Facebook automatically place your ads at certain spots, this is not always the right strategy to use. Facebook has an algorithm that determines where your ads would perform the best. That does not mean it will go as planned every time. Look at the placement menu to see what options are available and make a decision where you feel your ads would perform their best. Be willing to experiment now and again with different ad locations.

Read the Preview

After you have created your ad, you will get a full preview of what it will look. The layout will display your photo, how the text is organized, and any additional features that will appear around your ad. This lets you see if the ad looks precise and if everything is arranged so the data shows properly.

The preview features on Facebook are not device-specific. The ad might look different on a portable device depending on the browser, operating system, size of the screen, and so forth. Always consider that when getting your ads ready, especially as you are trying to produce a good layout.

You could always check on other devices to see how your ad layout appears. But that is completely optional and might take a while for you to do. Just look at how well the ad looks on your preview and imagine how it might look if it were compressed to a certain size.

Using the Power Editor to Create Ads

One smart idea for marketing on Facebook is to create ads that are unique and appealing using the use of the Facebook Power Editor. The Power Editor is a tool that lets you review everything taking place in your ad campaign.

The steps to use the Power Editor are the following:

1. Open the Power Editor.

2. Click on the Ads section.

3. Click to create a new ad.

4. Choose whether you want to work with a new campaign or if you want to just get the shell for a campaign set up. This latter option is just producing a structure for the ad.

5. Add information into the proper boxes relating to what the ad will feature.

6. Adjust the physical layout of individual features on the ad as needed. This includes the size of the photo, how much text will appear, where additional buttons are displayed, and so forth.

7. Click the Review Changes button to see how the ad looks.

8. Confirm the changes after reviewing, and the new ad should be produced correctly.

This setup gives you a bit of extra control over how your ads will be made and laid out. Regularly review how the ad is working according to the Power Editor.

Converting Existing Content into an Ad

You do not always have to create a new post or bit of media for an ad. You can always create a new ad featuring existing content on your page feed. This may work if you want to boost a post or if you feel the existing content is worthwhile and deserves to be read by more people. When the content is converted, it will appear with the post content showing a preview icon or a photo producing a link that goes to your site. You can preview your advertisement before you convert it into a new ad.

To convert current content into a new Facebook ad:

1. Go to the Ads Manager dashboard.

2. Click on the Use Existing Post option.

3. The menu will get you to your Facebook page. Review the posts on the page to determine which one you want to make into an ad.

4. Preview the advertisement to see if the post reads the way you want.

Check your entire feed to see what posts could be made into new advertising content. This could save you the trouble that comes with producing something new.

Adding Offer Ads

Offer ads are advertisements that let people see what offers you provide your customers. In some cases, an ad will include a description of a discount and a button that leads people to your website. It may also involve an invitation to visit your physical store. Depending on what you use, a promo code for your website may also be utilized in your ad.

Here is how you can create an offer ad:

1. Select the Traffic, Conversions and Store Visits option when looking at the objective for your ad in the Ads Manager tool.

2. Select the Offer option.

3. Select a page that you want to put your ad on.

4. Enter the specifics of your offer.

These include what the deal is for, how much it is worth, where to redeem the offer, and even a promo code or bar code if applicable.

5. Click on the Create button. You should get a preview of the ad.

6. Enter the proper details - who will see the ad, where it will be placed, and your budget for putting it online.

7. Determine the schedule that the offer ad will be listed online and enter it.

This is for ads where the deal will only be good for a certain time. You have the option to keep the ad up for as long as you want, but you should still think about how much of a demand people will have for it. So don't run the promotion into the ground.

8. Click on the Place Order button.

The ad should be approved and sent out to your target audience. This lets people know what you are promoting and what makes your offer exceptional.

Inserting a Promo Code

Some offers include promo codes that people enter on your website to take advantage of it. To use a promo code:

1. Go to the Offer Redemption section of the Create Offer screen.

2. Use the Unique Codes option.

3. Use the Upload CSV button to enter the file that includes the promo codes you wish to use.

The file should list parameters of the code you want to set up. This allows Facebook to read the data and generate a code that works exclusively for your offer. This is important if you want to offer a physical code that people can scan. The code has to be perfect and precise for scanning.

4. Click the Create button. Facebook will then produce ads that include the appropriate promo codes.

A CSV file is needed for your promo code, as it is what will program a code to work with a certain function on your site. With the wrong CSV, the promo code will not work properly. The good news is that the Facebook ad system will trigger proper actions to create a code that fits in with your site. Other than just using a CSV file, you do not have to do anything technical.

Inserting a Bar Code

A bar code may also work if your ad is for a physical retail location. Here are a few steps to use the bar code:

1. Use the same Unique Codes option on the Create Offer screen as is used for promo codes.

2. Upload your CSV or TXT file that includes details on all the bar codes you wish to use.

You will have to enter multiple bar code numbers into your file; a code generator that you can download elsewhere might help in this case.

3. Click on the Create button. Facebook should generate new bar codes based on the information you have sent in.

This process requires a bit of trial and error.

Should You Add Your Ads on Instagram?

Facebook has the option to put your advertisements on Instagram. This is thanks in part to Facebook owning a significant share of Instagram. The choice lets you get your messages out to more people on another social media platform. That does not mean you should click on the option that lets you add a post on Instagram.

Here are a few considerations when deciding if you should use Instagram alongside Facebook for certain posts:

- Both platforms are great for when you're trying to make people more aware of your work. The two are used for video and to print posts.

- Instagram and Facebook are appropriate together when you are trying to get people to download an app.

- Use Facebook without Instagram if you want people to engage in your app.

- Facebook alone works when you're trying to get people onto your website.

Remember that marketing on Facebook is different from doing the same on Instagram. This will be covered in a later chapter.

Overall, getting ads to work on Facebook is one of the best things to consider. Paid ads are perfect for helping people see what you have. Whether it is content going on your site or on someone else's page, you will have a setup that gets people to take action and engage with you.

Chapter 10 – District Types of Ads You Can Use on Facebook

Naturally, people think about pictures when it comes to advertisements. A vast majority of online ads are pictures, so that makes sense. However, you can do more than just use ordinary images. You can also format an ad to create a dynamic appearance where the images or messages produced might change. Facebook gives you the option to work with many kinds of advertisements to help you get your messages out in a unique and specific manner.

Working with special types of advertisements gives you the opportunity to work with any kind of point you want to express. You can use these options to illustrate anything whether it entails something vibrant or more detailed than what you might normally use. Just look at what is available, and you will come across an idea that gives you more out of the work you produce.

The formatting process gives you the option to use one of four selections for your ad:

1. A single image ad is the basic one you can work with.

2. A slideshow lets you display multiple images.

3. A video focusing on a full-motion video feature.

4. A carousel ad features many calls to action in one layout.

You have already learned about how to get a single image ad produced. Let's look at the other three options. Working with any of these three outstanding image options is always a good idea. They let you display some attractive items in different ways. It can be useful and distinct and should be explored.

You should still be careful about how you use them and what you plan on getting from these ads.

Slideshow

A slideshow ad is perfect for when you want to show people many things at one time. The slideshow is a series of images that are displayed over the course of a few seconds. The visitor will click on a button to start watching a series of images played out over a short time.

This option does well if you have several images that are linked together. Your images could produce a specific theme that people can quickly identify. For instance, a slideshow promoting an Italian restaurant can show many images of different Italian foods it might serve. Scenes of the atmosphere in the physical restaurant could be illustrated. The slideshow gives people a look at everything such a place has. It is difficult to incorporate multiple things into just one image; sometimes you need a full slideshow to make it stand out.

To produce a slideshow advertisement:

1. Go to the Ads Manager.

2. Choose an objective for the advertisement.

The slideshow option is not available for the catalog sales or post engagement objectives.

3. List the targeting and the budget.

4. Click on the Slideshow option in the Format section.

5. Click the Create Slideshow button.

6. Add a series of images that you want to illustrate in your slideshow. You drag these images to your slideshow from your hard drive.

When you add these images, you will have the option to sort them based on when they will appear. The bottom part of the screen will illustrate where the images are being displayed.

You can add up to ten images. Try to get as close to the maximum as possible, but be certain the pictures are relevant to your promotion.

7. Set the aspect ratio for the images. This is for showing how the image is to be laid out.

8. Choose the amount of time you will have each image appear on screen. Each slide can appear from 1 to 50 seconds.

9. List the transition you want to use. You can let your videos either fade into one another or not use a transition and let it appear as if each image is flashing.

10. Add music to your slideshow on the Music spot near the top.

You can upload your own music track or other audio track onto the slideshow if desired. You can also choose from one of many pre-made options produced by Facebook. This is useful providing that the music suits your video.

11. Edit individual photos if desired. You can add some text onto each slide.

The entire feature gives you an attractive advertisement you can use on Facebook to illustrate more things to the reader. Use the proper layout and think about the images that create a slideshow where everything fits perfectly.

Video

The next option for a Facebook ad is to produce a video. Video advertising is perfect because it lets you talk about anything in full motion. Sometimes a video might be more valuable than just a bunch of photos illustrating what you want to advertise. A quality video can be played on any mobile device that uses the Facebook app.

Here are the steps to produce a great video:

1. Go to the Ads Manager.

2. Select the Video option.

3. Choose a video that you want to upload onto your site.

The video should have already been made. You can upload the video from your hard drive or other storage device you are using.

Make sure the video is the proper format. Fortunately, Facebook supports an immense variety of formats. These include the.mpeg, mp4,.mov,.wmv,.vob,.qt,.divx and.gif, among others. The.mp4 and.mov formats are the ones Facebook recommends as the playback feature on the network runs with close to the same standards.

4. Analyze the layout of the video. Watch how it appears in a preview box.

5. Adjust the timing of the video based on when you want it to start and when it will end.

The bottom part of the screen includes a section to determine when and where the video will stop. Although it is best to do this with a video editor beforehand, you can still use this feature when you upload your video.

Tips for Producing Videos

As great as a video can be, you must be careful when producing one for your Facebook ad. Here are a few tips to use for getting a Facebook ad video ready:

- Keep your video as short as possible. A video ad that is 15 seconds long or less will be easier for people to watch till the end.

- Use a good physical layout for your video where the image is aligned properly. A landscape layout is best as it can be read on more devices that are mobile.

- Use a quality camera to produce your video. It should not be hard to find a high-definition camera that is light in weight and stable.

- The video will be played back on a square screen in most cases. This is to make it easier to read and to divide the video from any database.

- Maintain a consistent amount of sound coming from of your video. Use stock music in the background if you can. This is much more appealing than nothing playing in the background. Nevertheless, be sure you have the rights to use the music track you want to play in your video.

Technical Features of the Video

Your video must also be technically useful. That is, it needs to have a layout where it will be easy to read. The following technical points on your video are strongly recommended:

- Keep the aspect ratio at less than 1280 pixels wide. The Facebook player can only produce videos that are of a certain size.

- Let the aspect ratio be divisible by 16 pixels. This is to let it work on many mobile devices with smaller screens.

- Watch for the frame rate. A frame rate of 30 frames per second or less is best. Facebook does not work well with videos with a faster frame rate.

Make sure when getting quality videos produced that you know how to make them stand out and look their best. Your videos for your Facebook ads are important to be laid out properly, so they look their best. Keep your videos looking great and see that you are producing ones that fit perfectly with your marketing demands.

Carousel

The other special option for getting your ads online is to use the Carousel format. This format lets you show as many as ten videos or photos. It can also display headlines, links, or other messages you want to use. Think of the Carousel as an option that lets you use a variety of ad messages that can display many fun things at once.

With a Carousel, you can highlight a specific type of product you want to sell or a full range of products. You can use individual features on a Carousel to explain very specific or unique features of your products. You can even tell a full story through a series of cards with each spot coming forward in the narrative. There is also the option to show one very long panoramic image through a Carousel provided the images are connected with one another.

The ad creation tool will help you with producing a Carousel. Here are some steps you can use for getting this ready:

1. Choose the proper objective for your campaign in the Ads Manager.

You can only work with a Carousel if you want to get people to your website, increase the number of conversions on your site, get more video views, or get people to install your app. Choose one of these options depending on the results you wish to obtain.

2. Select the multiple images option on the Ad Format.

3. Check the box in the Images and Links section that refers to the best images and links you can work with at the given time.

This option lets you post bits of media to work in your Carousel. If you prefer, you can unclick the box to add other media. However, leaving it checked allows Facebook to scan for the best performing items on your site might be, thus giving you extra control over your work.

4. While on the Images and Links section, upload the images you want and enter particular URLs and descriptions.

5. Repeat with any other images or links you want to add.

This should let you get the Carousel sufficiently formed with the content you want to work with. As with the slideshow, the Carousel must have enough images that relate to the content of your site.

Creating a Carousel With the Power Editor

The Power Editor feature can also help you produce a good Carousel. Here are some steps for getting the Power Editor work for you:

1. Create a campaign with the proper objective in mind.

Like with the Ads Manager, you will select an objective before you start working. Choose the option to get clicks onto your website, get conversions, invite more app installs, get more engagement for the ad, get more video views, or to gather leads for your business. The mobile app engagement option is only available with the Power Editor.

2. Create a few ads that you want to produce.

3. Go to the Create Ad section on the editing tool.

4. Select the option to create a carousel layout for many images and videos.

5. Click on the number of cards you will use in the layout.

6. Add in the approximate price for each image in this carousel.

7. Use the Creative Optimization section to organize the images and links based on what might perform best.

Planning Your Carousel

The Carousel might be versatile and capable of supporting many images, but you must be cautious when getting it ready. A few things can be done to help you construct a fine layout:

- See how relevant the things you put on your Carousel are. They should blend in well with each other so people can go through the entire reel.

- Keep the Carousel as long as it needs to be without being stretched. You can use up to ten items but you it is fine to use less.

- Watch how the images and other features you put on your Carousel appear. They should all be of the same quality.

- Everything needs to be formatted with the same style, theme, color, lighting, and even attitude. Try not to go from one extreme to the next within the same Carousel. That might be too jarring for some readers.

Your Carousel will stand out and offer a fine layout provided you are careful with how you produce it. Be particular about how it will be organized.

Watch for What Appears First

The great thing about the Carousel is that you can adjust it in any way you see fit. You can get certain videos or photos to appear at the very start before the carousel moves around. This means you can choose what is to be seen first in the layout.

Choose what people will see before anything else. Make sure the layout is attractive from the beginning. When someone sees a great Carousel image at the start, they will be motivated to look at the entire carousel. That person will start to notice all the other features on the screen and will get a closer and more purposeful look at what you feature.

Review the Pricing for the Carousel

The next point for the Carousel to observe is that every image or video added will vary in cost. You might have to spend more money on clicks or impressions parts of the carousel than others.

Notice how each part of the layout is organized based on what you might spend on it. You might have to get the more expensive part of the Carousel to appear first simply because it most likely lead to conversions. Consider your daily budget to ensure your carousel will stay visible for a longer time.

You can always adjust the layout of the carousel so that certain parts will appear later while others will be closer to the start. Don't ignore the pricing, so you have more control over how well it is arranged and utilized.

Targeting People With Older Devices

Your ads must be capable of reaching an audience on many platforms. These include people who use Facebook on their mobile devices. The problem with some devices is that they are old or operating on smaller networks. Some people are not able to afford devices that play back the media you are using.

Fortunately, you can adjust the individual media ads so that they appear only on very specific devices. The detailed targeting feature on Facebook lets you choose where your media campaigns can appear.

To target your ads toward certain devices:

1. Open the Ads Manager.

2. Review each individual advertisement you are listing. Click on whichever one you wish to alter.

3. Go to the targeting section of the ad.

4. Review the settings based on which devices are likely to review your ads.

5. Adjust the settings so people who have certain devices or newer ones will see your ads if they are technically substantial.

6. Choose to limit your ads to screens of a certain size.

7. Review the online connection one uses to get online. Adjust your ads to target people who use devices that reach particular networks.

Complete this for every ad set you have.

A good rule of thumb is to use as many of these types of ads as possible. This way, you will have one version of an advertisement appearing on a certain device or network and a different version showing up on another device. Making sure this works makes it easier to get your work promoted.

Chapter 11 – How Much Money Should You Spend on Facebook Ads?

Like with any other online advertising venture, you need to spend money for some of the Facebook ads. The total amount that you spend will vary based on whom you wish to target and how to make your site visible. The good news is that you can set a budget for how much money you want to spend on Facebook ads. Once you set the budget, your ads will stop after a certain length of time. You must plan everything carefully if you want the best possible campaign to work for you.

What Does It Cost?

The fee to advertise on Facebook is based on how much money it costs when someone clicks on an ad. With Facebook, the amount of money you spend is influenced by the total you will pay for each click or for every thousand of impressions. This is important for your success, as you need to get enough money to make your campaign visible.

You might spend 50 cents per click on your ad. This means that you will have to pay 50 cents every time someone clicks on your advertisement. You do not pay to get your ad online if no one clicks on the ad. However, you could spend lots of money if more people find your ad and actually click it.

You might have to pay for every thousand impressions an ad gets. An impression is an instance where someone reads your advertisement. This would mean that your ads appear on a screen for enough people to read the ad based on what you are spending on it. This is good when you just want a little more exposure or name recognition.

One point about marketing worth mentioning involves the exposure that your ad will get. Your ad might get thousands of views but not too many clicks. But as you get more views, the potential for you to have more clicks will increase. It is estimated that about 1 to 2 percent of people who view a Facebook ad will actually click on it. That number might be even lower when it targets a smaller group.

The specific total you spend on each ad will vary based on many factors:

- The industry you are in; you might spend more if you are in an industry with a larger demand.

- The overall size of your audience; Facebook can review your work to see how large your audience might be.

- The overall quality of your ad; something with a little more detail to it might cost extra.

- The time of year when you buy an ad; a business dealing with outdoor basketball equipment might spend more on an ad during the summer when people are likely to play that sport.

Overall, you might spend around 30 to 50 cents for each click on your ad. This is a sensible total to spend as it relates to the click-through ratio on your ad. Plan your budget based on the overall clicks your ad might get. Remember that your ad is not going to appear any longer if you have gone beyond the set budget.

Some professional groups, particularly fashion lines and movie studios, could spend several dollars for each click. They would spend that money just to make their content more visible. Such entities could still afford to spend all that money on the campaign. This makes your efforts for planning an ad with a good budget and a focused target reach all the more essential.

Getting a Budget Ready

The process for getting a marketing effort running on Facebook is easy. A few simple steps can help you get a budget laid out:

1. After producing an advertisement that you want to display and choosing the audience, you will be sent to a menu on the Ads Manager listing your budget and schedule.

2. Review the daily budget you wish to spend on the ads.

The daily budget is what you will spend each day on your advertising. A total that limits your spending. Once that budget is reached, the ads will stop appearing on Facebook until the next day when it resets.

3. Select the schedule. You can get it to work as long as you want or with a certain range of days.

You can get your ad to run continuously for as long as needed. There is also the option to have a start and end date for your campaign. Scrutinize with care as a continuous campaign will have no limit to how much you would spend (although the daily limit still applies).

4. Determine whether you want to use a CPC or CPM payment setup.

A CPC or Cost Per Click setup is what you will spend for one click on an ad. The CPM or Cost Per Mile is the cost per thousand impressions or views. The CPC option is best when you are trying to get people onto your Facebook page or website. The CPM is to make your work more visible.

5. Add a general bid for what you will spend for a CPC or CPM campaign.

For this step, you must list how much you are willing to spend for each click or thousand views. A specific total should be added based on what you feel your work is worth plus your budget. Typically, you have to pay around 50 cents per click or for a certain number of views.

After you get the timing and budget ready, you will get a calculation from Facebook on what the maximum cost of your campaign will be. You might not even spend the full amount unless you reach the maximum number of clicks allowed in your campaign. Plan your campaign with care; you never know how many people are going to click on your links. Be attentive of any sudden boosts in the popularity of your work. Your content could be so popular that your ad will have a short run time before it is removed for the day.

What About Boosted Posts?

Boosted posts are easy to find. They are the ads that appear at the very top of a search on Facebook. This is what you might see on a search engine when something appears prominently after you enter a keyword. While boosted posts can be rather appealing, you will have to be careful about how much they cost.

A boosted post typically appears when someone spends more money on a post. The person who puts the most money toward a keyword will get their post boosted. This adds to the exposure of the ad.

To set up a boosted post:

1. Identify the specific post you want to boost.

2. Click on the Boost Post button.

3. Determine the audience you want to target.

4. Enter details on the budget and how long the ad will appear online.

5. Select your payment option to pay Facebook for the ads you are producing.

Not all posts can be boosted as ads. Some older content or expired data cannot be promoted. Facebook does not support some app install posts, video posts and other bits of multimedia content for ad boosting either.

Watch for the demand that comes with your ad. While you might reach many people, that post will stop once you reach the daily spending limit on your campaign. Be prepared to spend a little extra on your daily budget to make your ad more visible to a larger audience during the life of your campaign.

Chapter 12 – Working With Facebook Analytics

Be attentive to your Facebook marketing efforts. This is where Facebook Analytics or Facebook Insights can work for you. Analytics assists you with discovering where your site is going and how people are accessing or using it. The details you will get should explain what makes your site worthwhile.

The analytics reports lend a full understanding of what you are doing properly and what needs improvements. This includes a look at which ads people are clicking on or what parts of your site are the most popular. Analytics reports change all the time and can be based on when certain things took place. Using the analytics feature on your Facebook page is vital to your success.

How to Review Your Engagement Rate

There are a few simple steps to follow when getting Facebook Analytics to work for you:

1. Click on the Insights section on the top part of your page.

2. Click on the Posts section.

3. Go to the All Posts Published section to review everything.

4. Click on the arrow right of the post clicks section. This gives you a list of all the things you can review.

5. Select the Engagement Rate option.

This will list information about how often people engage with your site. Use this to examine things like:

- How many people clicked on a post.

- How often people forward your work.

- The number of comments people are posting.

All of these things are measured based on when they take place. This gives you a clear idea of what people are doing when visiting your page. You can use this to decide what content is popular versus what needs to be improved.

Choosing the Boost Option

The choice to use the Boost option is available on any post that you review. You can use the engagement rate check to gain access to this button. When getting the engagement statistics, click on the Boost button to promote a post. This will lead you to the standard budgeting menu.

Checking Likes and Unlikes

Get plenty of likes for not only your site but also for individual posts. The process for checking the likes on your page and posts is as follows:

1. Go to the Analytics menu as listed above.

2. Click on the Likes tab.

3. Review the range on the screen. This shows your page's performance over a time. You can change the dates on the range to look at specific things posted.

4. Review the total number of likes on the screen based on the range you have selected.

As you evaluate this information, you will get reports on the workings of your page. You will find information on likes based on:

- How people like your ads.

- Things on your page that people like.

- Whether people like any page suggestions that come up on your site; this could give you ideas of what your viewers like.

- How people like search results.

You might notice that a large number of likes on your site are coming from your ads. This might mean you should work more on your ads to make them more visible. This is because the ads are more attractive to people and bring them to visit your site.

While all this is useful, you should use the same process for unlikes as well. People might choose to unlike your page for whatever reason. Those can reveal information on what makes your site unpopular with some individuals. Using the analytics to discover where unlikes are coming from and where they appear will help to resolve the problem.

Review the Reach

The reach on your Facebook Analytics report refers to something different from the views on your ad. Although the views can help you see how often people are getting to some parts of your page, the reach is even more important. This refers to how many people have seen your work on their news feeds. A place that has a larger reach is always one that shows how widespread your work is.

The reach will give you ideas on what is happening on your site based on how people are coming online. The details you find are important to give you the setup you desire for your site.

Review the People Section

One critical point about Facebook Analytics involves the People section. This is the part of your Insights that looks into the people who are getting onto your site. It lists information on people based on many critical demographics. This information can help you understand why people visit your site. The People section will list information like:

- Men and women and how they access the site.

- The age groups that your viewers belong to; this is divided by gender.

- Specific locations through which people reach your work.

- The languages that people are using in their searches.

You can use the People section to analyze who visits your site based on these features:

- The fans who actually like your page.

- The number of people you have reached.

- How many people were engaged; how many people have accessed your page.

- Check-ins, if applicable.

Can You Use Other Programs?

The option to work with a different program for your analytics needs exists. Various groups offer their own analytics services that help to look at your data in a simplified and useful manner. HootSuite is one of the options when seeking help with your work. Search to find others as you see fit. This will help in being able to use other programs.

Take a look at your Facebook Analytics reports often to see what you can learn and take appropriate action to correct shortfalls. All of what you utilize and do will help you address and control issues of planning your Facebook ads.

Chapter 13 – Using Facebook Live

With Facebook, you can do more than post messages. You can also produce videos and share them. Moreover, today you can do more than just post videos on a feed. You can also stream a video for people to interact with in real time. All thanks to Facebook Live.

Facebook Live is a special way to communicate with others online. With Facebook Live, you can interact with people in real time with a video camera. Record and stream something, then respond to people who leave messages on your video feed. It all works in a seamless and simple layout accessible on any device that works with Facebook.

Facebook Live allows you to speak directly to people and share unique contemplations. It could also be useful at a live event, and you want to share the experience with someone. This might be a board meeting, an event at a convention, or something else about your business. You only need to get the live event set up on Facebook.

The best part of this is that Facebook Live is free to use so long as you have a proper video camera to work with. Considering how high-definition cameras are cheap and portable these days, it should not be hard for you to get online and market your work to others through Facebook Live without having to spend a lot of money.

Facebook Live has already become a hit with many big-name celebrities. Sports personalities like Tony Hawk and Lindsey Vonn, celebrities such as Ricky Gervais and Michael Buble, and journalists including Jorge Ramos have been using Facebook Live to interact with people and to answer questions they might have. People want to talk with people they admire and will certainly go to Facebook to follow their favorites and what's happens in their lives. You can use Facebook Live to help you interact with whoever might have an interest in your work.

Think of Facebook Live as if it were a version of Twitch produced for the Facebook world. Twitch has been popular for live streaming videos although they focus more on e-sports. Facebook Live is essentially live streaming brought to the public at large.

This chapter is about looking how to get Facebook Live work for you. The interactivity and real-time nature of Facebook Live makes it one of the most exciting ways to share information and ideas with other people with a special platform that you are bound to love using.

How to Start a Facebook Live Event

It is easy to get your own Facebook Live event organized. These steps will give you the best control over your own unique event.

1. Go to the News feed on your page.

2. Click on the Live button. This should be listed with a camcorder icon.

3. Choose the privacy setting.

The privacy setting you use will send your feed only to those who like your page or are in a group you have set up. You can also make your feed available to anyone. Review what you want to do with your event and whether you want it open to the public or not.

4. Write a description for the event.

The description is the text that goes next to the event title. This should attract the reader or viewer.

5. Use some tags for your feed.

The Facebook Live setup menu will list information on the tags you can add. You can choose to work with one of many tags including ones based on specific friends, activities you want to highlight, your current or planned location, etc. Have a clear idea of what you want to present.

6. Prepare the camera.

The camera should be connected to whatever device you are using to access Facebook. In most cases, the camera will be something built into a Smartphone or tablet. You could also get a larger high-definition camera attached to your device if desired.

The camera has to produce a clear image that is distinguishable and have good audio. You could add a separate microphone to create a newscast-like approach to your video if you want.

Try to use a separate HD camera that attaches to a computer or other device instead of an integrated camera in a tablet or on a phone. The outside camera will more than likely have a better resolution level than what is found in a tablet or on a phone.

7. Click on-the-Go Live button when you are ready.

What to Do During the Recording

There are some extra things todo while the actual recording process. Some of these make your video a little more dynamic. Other options create a fun look to what you want to produce.

The following options are viable choices to have when getting your Facebook Live experience become more exciting:

1. Check the additional effects you can add to your video.

The effects you apply to your video can include special lenses, filters, and other features that create dynamic visual charm. This could add a fun appearance if used correctly.

2. Add text to your video.

A text feature could be included at the bottom part of the screen. Send out a message that you want people to see as soon as they can get online. Create text that is simple to read. This is to make your work easier to follow.

3. Check the comments that come along.

A great part of using Facebook Live is that you can incorporate great comments from other people as you work. With Facebook Live, you can respond to anything that someone wants to tell you. Instead of typing something, you can give a more detailed response to any comment as you're recording.

You will solicit these questions from others as you work. Make sure you get enough remarks to make it easier for the video to be active and useful. A Facebook Live session will be more fun when you are interactive, or you are sharing things with other people.

The comments always appear in reverse chronological order. In this case, the most recent comments will appear at the top while the oldest ones are at the bottom. You can always navigate through the comments at any time and review them as needed.

4. Notice the various emojis that appear on the screen.

The bottom part of the screen near the live comments will show you various emojis. These are added around the screen to let you know what people are thinking about your work. The emojis you will see include everything from a thumbs-up to a smiling face, even a crying face, and many others.

The things you will see on these emojis will be posted on the screen as viewers are watching. Survey them when they appear, so you get an idea of how your viewers are reacting.

5. Be prepared to block anyone on your Live session.

There is always the potential for someone to get onto Facebook Live to troll people, hassle others, or be abusive. Watch out for them as they will get in the way and hurt the overall experience. To block a viewer, tap the profile photo next to a person's remark and then select the Block option.

You also have the option to unblock people on your feed. You would have to touch that person's profile on the comment line again to unblock that person. Be cautious because you do not want to be too abusive or inflexible in any situation.

Always look at what you can do when using Facebook Live. See how well you share things with others and have a good plan of what you wish to express in any situation.

After the Feed is Over

After you are finished with your feed, you can save it so people can watch it later. This is ideal for trying to get your work out to more people. After all, it is not as though everyone can get onto Facebook Live to see it right away.

After the feed is complete, click on the Finish button. This ends the live feed and brings you to a new menu. Once completed, you will be given one of many options:

1. You can click the Post button to get your feed posted on your page. This will let people watch the video.

2. You could also click the Delete button to discard the entire feed. This works best when you have a feed that is time sensitive and cannot be used for anything else.

3. The Download button also allows you to get a copy of the feed downloaded onto your hard drive. You can get a full copy so you can protect it in the event that the feed is lost or unavailable for any particular reason.

Working with your feed after it is over is not difficult to make it available to a bigger audience.

Using Facebook Live With a Desktop Computer

It is best to use a mobile device to market yourself on Facebook Live as they have a camera feature that lets you record things and promptly send them out. You have the option to use Facebook Live with a desktop computer if you prefer. Get a Facebook Live setup started with a desktop computer if you want to record in just one place. This is best when working with a single static shot and a good video file.

For instance, you can use a Facebook Live post on a desktop if you have a conference in a convention hall or other places where such a meeting might occur. Here, the camera does not move around and go from one spot to the next.

That works best if you have proper AV equipment attached to your computer. You can quickly get a camera attached to your desktop computer. A microphone can be added too although you may have to pass it to others in some scenarios.

The good news is that you can work with much AV equipment to get your Facebook Live activity recorded on a desktop computer. Test everything beforehand to see that it works correctly. Make sure you look at how well the desktop is arranged to make it easy for viewers to follow.

You will definitely have a better quality stream when you work with a desktop computer. There are no worries about the camera shaking or the audio possibly cutting in and out as you move around. Still, plan the live event carefully. Make sure the setup works and that you have the best possible equipment on hand to record your event.

When to Use Facebook Live

Facebook Live is best to use when you have plans for the following:

- Question-and-answer sessions. Invite people to your feed and answer questions relating to anything you want to market.

- Conferences where you are going to discuss what your business is doing.

- Remote trips. You can travel to many different spots while recording your actions on a mobile device.

- Special events at your physical place of work. You can use a camera to record whatever is happening at that moment.

- You can stream activities. Watch activities with others provided that you are cautious. For instance, you could stream watching a sporting event with someone.

- Demonstrations of a product or service you are offering. This could help you with illustrating the particulars of a product.

Facebook Live is an exciting option when you want to market your business. With this, you can leverage streaming videos to your advantage.

How Long Should a Live Session Be?

There is a four-hour limit for Facebook Live sessions. You can make your experience as short as you want or up to four hours. Plan your sessions carefully based on how much time you want to spend and what you want your window of connectivity to be.

Stay online for at least ten minutes. This should be enough time to say what you want while responding to your viewers.

Having a longer session allows you to talk with more people and to answer more questions. You will also have a larger window of opportunity for people to talk to you. Facebook Live offers support of chats of up to four hours in length.

Key Tips For Using Facebook Live

There are a few things you can do to ensure you get the most out of your Facebook live experience:

1. Tell people when you will be going online.

Let people know about your Facebook Live experience ahead of time. You could make an event out of it and promote it a few times on your regular Facebook page. Just make the occasion something special that you want to share with your followers.

2. Make sure your online connection is strong.

A Facebook Live post will work with a strong connection. This includes something with 4G support if possible. You must have a better connection so you can support a good picture and audio setup. People will appreciate your work if you can keep yourself online without being at risk of having the online link disconnect. The 4G setup also ensures you have a clear image and sound signal while moving. This also lets you read comments in real time as they appear on the screen.

3. Produce a good description.

Always create a description that is intriguing and invites people to tune in. You need to draw in people before they click onto your link. Let them know what you offer is interesting and worth looking into.

4. Interact with your followers.

Pay attention to the comments people send. Respond to those followers so they will continue connecting with you. They want to know that you pay attention to them and you will respond when they send messages. People will especially love it when they get direct responses from you because they know you value what they say and shows that you care about them and their opinions.

Always refer to the people you are responding to by name. This tells others who you are responding to. It also lets them know that you value what they say. Being detailed shows that you are aware of all your readers and that you say something special to whoever might be following you on your feed.

5. Always use a good closing line.

Use a proper closing line at the end of your Live session. The line could let people know to visit you at a certain website or to see your regular Facebook page or any other social media site you have. You could even tell people when you will be available in the future. Afterwards, click the Finish button and listen for the ping to let you know when your Live session is officially ended.

Avoid Anything Illegal

Make sure that you do not engage in foul or difficult actions. You have to follow the proper conduct standards that Facebook has incorporated into its system. These rules are to ensure you use the correct behavior while avoiding anything that might be risky or otherwise illegal.

Avoid streaming anything that is unlawful to stream. One problem with many live streaming functions is that people often use them to help people pirate things that they should be paying for. This was especially noticeable in 2015 when people using various live streaming programs aired a boxing match between Floyd Mayweather and Manny Pacquiao that had been rumored and hyped for years. Instead of paying money to see this event, people were going to live streaming sites to see the session free.

This is illegal as people are supposed to be paying for access to things like concerts, movie premieres, boxing and combat sport events, and many other shows. You might think people will be interested in your videos as you attend a big event but the odds are you might be doing something illegal if you are streaming it without the producer's permission.

Avoid any criminal actions on your Facebook Live streams. You obviously do not want to do anything sexual or harmful during your stream. People can report your work to Facebook if they see anything problematic.

Remember that working with Facebook Live can help you to make your work visible and interesting to more people. Being able to interact with your followers is always great. Be careful how you invite those followers to get in touch with you and that you are cautious about getting them all online.

Chapter 14 – Vital Considerations for Using Facebook for Marketing Purposes

Your work with Facebook for marketing will pay off if handled right. To make it useful and valuable, be careful about how you use Facebook. There are several practical things to think about as you aim to use Facebook for your marketing.

Remember That Your Work is for Business

You should use Facebook for highlighting your business, not your personal self. While you can always talk about yourself on your own profile; your business is the focal point of your marketing. Avoid doing something that might not be connected to your business. Show people that you have a strong investment and interest in your business and that you want to focus on it above all else.

Keep Every Image You Use Recognizable

Facebook relies on images. You can use images in any way you see fit, but it is vital to look at how the images you use are organized. Keep the images ready to be used. Even more importantly, they must be ones that readers will understand and recognize. Pictures are messages that the reader will not need help to decipher or analyze.

Review each image you post and see if they are easy to recognize. Don't use pictures that are complicated or confusing to anyone who is not familiar with whatever you offer.

Respond to Messages Often

One thing you might notice when looking at other Facebook pages is that they have badges showing how quickly they respond to messages. A page that has a badge with a speech bubble with some speed lines on it is one that responds to feedback or comments often and quickly.

Today you can get a badge showing that you take quick action in a few steps:

1. Check the comments on your page frequently to see what people are saying.

You might need to respond to some of them depending on the message.

2. Look for any questions that people send to you. These include questions from posts linked directly onto your site.

Some people might ask about how a business is run or what you provide. They could ask about specific products or services you highlight. Anything should be reviewed and answered as soon as possible.

3. Look at trends relating to what people are saying.

You can post new messages that relate to whatever people are saying. Show that you understand what people are talking about and that you care about their needs. Think about certain messages that indicate a trend developing. See what people say and show that you understand the issues they have.

By responding in a prompt and quick manner, you will prove your audience that you understand their concerns and needs. Do this regularly to demonstrate your interest and that you value your audience.

Include Milestones

You read earlier about milestones and how they can be used on your page. But what are these milestones?

Milestones are made to show people what makes your business special. Milestones will list information on things like:

- When your business was formed.

- When significant people entered into your business and what they accomplished.

- New products or services you introduced.

- Expansion of your business.

- Significant landmarks regarding sold products or services.

Milestones are great to add as they illustrate that your business has been around for some time. You can get these added to the About section to share what you have been doing and that your work is important. This is great for showing people what makes your work outstanding and valuable.

All of these solutions for using Facebook for marketing purposes are valuable points to follow. Use them well, so it becomes easier to market your work and make it useful to your audience. You will be impressed how well Facebook works for marketing.

Chapter 15 –YouTube

Another highly valuable option for social media marketing is YouTube. It is one of the top places to visit online. In fact, YouTube has become a very popular place in recent times thanks to how it highlights videos of all descriptions.

Perhaps you have been entertained by various videos on YouTube recently. Maybe you visited YouTube to find a how-to video or something informative or educational. You could look to YouTube to find older entertainment videos from years ago that you have not seen for some time.

These videos might have been forwarded. It is actually something noteworthy for your marketing as numerous of the best videos online are forwarded many times over. You could make a video relating to your business forwarded to many on YouTube, thus giving you a better chance of having your work visible because so many people could find it by someone's recommendation.

YouTube can be incredibly valuable to your business. It will require producing videos that are exceptional and worth sharing.

YouTube was developed in 2005 in California. It was introduced as a means of inviting people online to watch streaming videos of all kinds. With this, people can watch videos without using other programs. They just have to use a web browser with a proper plug-in that allows them to watch a video.

The popularity of YouTube caught on quickly as many things were being added. Performance videos, historic archival videos, and other things were posted on YouTube. Advertisements of all sorts started appearing including ones that highlight certain products or services. Even music videos became popular on YouTube.

Over the years, YouTube has grown and now offers videos of all kinds. Regardless of what you are interested in, the odds are you will be more visible if you get on YouTube and post an interesting video.

Musicians are using YouTube to post music videos and live performances. Small businesses are displaying videos of what they offer and even some how-to videos. Sports teams are posting videos that show interviews with players, team highlights, and much more. You can create videos that show what you are doing or explain to people something that could change their life for the better.

How the Technology Works

YouTube works with a simple format that allows people to play back videos. Any video file that is uploaded onto YouTube will be converted to the VP9 or H.264/MPEG-4 AVC format. These standard formats support high-definition viewing and are easy to load. The conversion process for these files ensures the data in those videos will be kept intact and not be at risk of being lost in the process.

The most important feature of this is that it all works with the HTML5 format. This means that videos can be streamed on a web browser or mobile device with ease. There is no need to download Flash, a plug-in that YouTube used to work with. Of course, a browser will still need to work with HTML5 although it should not be difficult to find an appropriate plug-in if necessary.

The YouTube system also operates well with mobile playback features. It has its own special application that lets people view videos on the go. This can work with almost any mobile operating system. The fact that such apps are easy to download or operate only makes them easier to work with. Simply put, YouTube can be used by many people anywhere. The universal setup of YouTube and its ability to be used on mobile devices make it valuable to anyone who wants to market something. It only makes sense that you would use YouTube to get the word out on anything you want to highlight to others.

Who Uses YouTube?

The demographics of those who use YouTube are important to notice. In particular, YouTube is a vast place that features channels of all sorts. Some people have channels that highlight what professional sports teams are doing. Other channels offer how-to videos on home improvement. Just type in a keyword and you will find something worth reviewing.

In fact, you will reach a large number of people when using YouTube. It is estimated that around four-fifths of all Americans have access to YouTube. This does not mean that all them are on YouTube regularly. However, there are a few things of interest to note:

- Most people who use YouTube are in the 25-34 age groups.

- About one billion people use YouTube every day from more than a hundred countries.

- ComScore says that around two-thirds of all people who use YouTube use it on their mobile devices. This is vital for when you are trying to reach people over an extended line.

- The things men and women look for are radically different. Women who use YouTube typically look for stuff on cosmetics, skin care, weight loss, and pop music. Men typically look for information on video games, sports, and bodybuilding. This is according to a 2015 OpenSlate report.

Why Use YouTube?

YouTube has clearly become a popular place to visit for many reasons. You might be concerned that it is difficult to get a video recorded and ready to use. However, you will see that YouTube is easy to use. There are many attractive things that make YouTube special:

Free to Advertise

Get on YouTube without having to pay a single penny to advertise. You have the option to enter a special campaign that will cost money to get your ads to appear in certain spots. You will have pay to get the proper recording equipment. You could record with a mobile device, but it is best to opt for a more professional approach to record your content.

Give People More to See

With YouTube, you can show people more than just a static image or a brief clip. You can use YouTube to promote anything with a full motion video setup. Your video could include several minutes of something that you might want to illustrate to others. The video can be up to 15 minutes in length, although you can record shorter videos.

Creativity Reigns Supreme

You have the right to produce all kinds of videos on YouTube. You can target people with any kind of content you want so long as it does not violate the terms that YouTube has posted. These include rules relating to what you own or whether the things you are posting are appropriate for people to watch. Use your best judgment. Make your videos unique.

Great for SEO Purposes

One reason why social media marketing is popular is the use of search engine optimization. By posting a video on YouTube, you can create a description that includes a link to your business site. This adds a natural link that improves your site's SEO ranking. As a result, people will have an easier time spotting something on your page. Including a transcript of your video could help you be ranked higher on a search engine.

YouTube is also linked to Google Plus, thus making it easier for you to market your work on Google. The prominent search engine has a huge share in YouTube. This means YouTube videos often appear at the top of searches. More importantly, the link you produce on your YouTube video will be easier for a Google search spider to find. This improves how easily people will spot your video.

People Stay on YouTube Longer

People who visit YouTube are more likely to stay on the site for a longer time than on other social media sites. Shareaholic states that individuals will visit around three YouTube pages in one typical visit. This is close to one more page than what people might visit elsewhere. People spend at least four minutes on the site each time they visit, which is much longer than on other sites. This might be due to how long some videos are. This does suggest that people are more likely to stay on a site to find videos than any other social media sites.

Not Too Technical

The interface used by YouTube is very simple. It lets you take any video file you have created and get it ready for use online.

The interface for uploading and editing videos is simple to follow. Details on how the editing interface on YouTube works will be covered later in this guide. It is easy to edit, as you will see. YouTube has various settings you can use to adjust your videos to make them striking and attractive.

Ideas For What You Can Post on YouTube

You have the freedom to post whatever you want on YouTube. Some of these videos include the following:

- Illustrate to viewers how a particular product or service works.

- Display the features of what you have for sale in a clear and direct manner.

- Post interviews with people involved in your business.

- Post historic information relating to your work. This might include a look at your business' evolution and anything that might have influenced your business.

- Post live events and remote recordings to be shared with others. You can even use YouTube for live streaming, which will be covered in a later chapter.

Feel free to experiment with different types of content.

Pitfalls of YouTube

As great as YouTube is for social media marketing, it does have a few drawbacks. The following are a few of the points you should be looking into when getting YouTube to work for you.

Not Much Control Over the Presentation

The screen layout that YouTube has for presenting videos is consistent on all platforms. Although YouTube can adjust videos into different resolution levels, you can only go so far with your video over how well it can be presented. The general layout that YouTube uses on its player is optimized for mobile devices and smart television sets. Therefore, you have to produce a video that would look like something designed to air on one of them. Those using a desktop or laptop computers will see it in the same way. However, they could expand the video to cover an entire screen.

Your Videos Have to Be Marketed

You will still have to market your videos to make people notice them. Although you can use a good listing on your video to make it easier to find on a YouTube search, you might have to promote your videos on other social media sites. You need to post a link to your video on different social media pages that you own or ones that are relevant to what you have going. This is all about making your work easy to spot.

You can always use keywords in your title, a description, and other features to make your work noticeable. This will help people who search for certain concepts find your video above all else. Even with that, you have to look at how well your marketing efforts are organized, so it becomes easier for you to make your work discernible.

The Value Isn't Always Recognized

You might be thrilled that you are getting lots of views and upvotes on your YouTube video. But that does not mean people will actually visit your site or business location. Also, this does not guarantee people will forward your videos to others. In other words, people who get on the site will not necessarily respond to your call-to-action and do everything you ask them to do. This makes it more important for you to work on generating only the best possible videos and productions on YouTube.

All of these concerns are legitimate when you are marketing yourself on YouTube. Do not let these concerns make you shy away. The advantages of using YouTube are greater than any problems you might come across. All you have to do is come up with a great idea for a video and find a way to make it more visible.

YouTube is a valuable resource for marketing your business. With YouTube, you can get online and let people know all about what you have to offer. To make it work, you need to use the pointers listed in the next few chapters to give you the best experience possible.

Chapter 16 – What You Need For Advertising on YouTube

To start working with YouTube, you have to use several steps to help you get on the site and to produce videos. Fortunately, you can get everything ready easily.

Create a Profile

Get your own profile on YouTube ready at the start. To use YouTube you need to log into Google Plus. This is the system that Google uses to give access to various online services and to be listed on Google. It is typically a good idea for a business to register with Google and Google Plus just to add your contact information and other details, but also to use YouTube for marketing.

To get your profile set, do the following:

1. Register for a Google Plus profile.

You will have to go to the Google website and click on the Sign In button to create an account. Enter a user name, a password, and your current email address and other details. You will have to verify your account with a text to a mobile number. Then you can get onto YouTube to create your own channel.

The best thing to do is to get a brand account ready. A brand account is like a personal Google Plus profile but for businesses instead. You should upload your videos through your brand account so people can see what you have to offer. Refer to the Google Plus section of this book to see how to get a brand account set up.

2. As you get on YouTube, open the My Channel link on the left-hand side of the screen.

3. Click on the option to use a business or other name for your channel.

4. Enter the brand account name you wish to use.

5. Click on the About page.

6. Click the proper edit button on the page to enter details on what your site offers.

Be direct when telling people about the products and services you offer. Imitate the following points:

- Add keywords onto your page. This makes it easier to spot your work when a search is conducted. Make sure the keywords relate to what you are promoting.

- Explain who will post on the site and how often you might add things onto the page.

- Insert a few additional links. You can add links to other social media sites or your personal website.

7. Add a personal profile photo. Click on the small box on the top-left part of the screen to add an avatar photo. This is where people will see when you post things onto other pages.

Depending on what you entered into Google Plus, you might already have a profile photo listed. You can always change the photo if desired.

8. Add a header for your channel. Go to the top-right corner to open an option for changing the image you will display on that header. This is entered next to the avatar photo.

9. Go to the gear icon near the top-right part of the screen where the subscribe button is. Click and then choose to customize the layout of your channel.

Your channel page can be laid out in any way you want. Choose to add specific videos that you want to show first on a page. Additionally, sort between the view subscribers will see and what non-subscribers will notice. This lets you promote your work to others in a better light.

Get the Proper Equipment For Your Video

You could technically use a camera on a Smartphone or tablet to produce videos promoting your business on YouTube. That does not mean working with something rudimentary is a good option. The problem with such a small camera is that it will not pick up audio well. It won't produce a great picture either. You should use something a little more professional for the best results.

To get a video recorded:

1. Get a proper camera that can record well. A small high-definition camera is useful.

GoPro cameras are especially popular. Such cameras are becoming increasingly more affordable. Make sure that you know how to operate it.

2. Pay attention to the microphone feature on the camera. A camera needs to have a good microphone although a separate attachment might be needed if you have a smaller unit. Try to keep the microphone off-screen.

3. Look at the lighting you are using. Review how everything photographs so you can get a proper layout that looks great.

4. Look at the benefits of a video editing tool. Use it to produce a variety of special effects or overlays on your video.

You can employ various video editing programs for your YouTube video. Pinnacle Studio, Virtual Dub, and iMovie are among the top options. You could still edit features on your video directly through YouTube although it might be easier to take advantage of something more professional.

Uploading the Video

The process for recording and editing your video is clearly up to you. Next, pay attention to how you your video will be added onto YouTube.

To upload a video onto YouTube:

1. Click the download icon on the top-right part of the screen.

2. Select a video from your hard drive.

3. Enter the title and description.

The title should include a listing of what your video is about. It could include a keyword relating to the video's content.

The description is where you will add the detailed information on the video. It is also where you can place your business URL and other links.

4. Enter a series of tags.

The tags describe what is in the video. They can appear when someone is searching for your video. Use as many tags as you have to, but try to be specific. Refer to what you talk about in the video and location.

5. Click the social media links or other features that you use to share the video.

You can share your video on other sites by clicking the proper icons on the right-hand side of the upload screen. Share it on Facebook, Twitter, or other sites connected to your profile. You can also add a message through the platform to let people know to watch your video. (Don't forget that people who watch your video can use the YouTube player to forward a video to another social media site too.)

6. Select the thumbnail you want to use.

You can always choose a random slide from your video as a thumbnail that people will see before watching your video. You can also have your own custom thumbnail that you can upload.

7. Click on the Advanced Settings section to make some adjustments.

Enter many things on the Advanced Setting section to improve how your video works. Your video can allow the following features:

- The ability to post comments.

- The option to only display comments you approve.

- Allow users to leave ratings for your video.

- Distribution settings including the option to embed a video or to publish on a subscriber's page.

- Enable age restriction; this means that you will keep underage viewers from watching your videos although you cannot promote the video in an ad campaign.

- Select the category for your video; these include entertainment, how-to, and news categories.

8. Click the Publish button at the top-right corner of the screen to get the video uploaded. It should be fully accessible to all.

Editing Your Video Through YouTube

Although a video editor can help you before you upload your video to YouTube, there might be times when you have to edit a video after it is online. This is due to YouTube's system possibly affecting the general quality of the video. Maybe you might even find an issue that you want to resolve, but you never noticed it until after you uploaded your video. Fortunately, YouTube does have its own feature to edit videos. Use this feature if you need extra help to make the video more attractive.

To edit your videos:

1. Go to the Creator Studio on your YouTube channel.

2. Click on the Edit button on the specific video that you want to edit.

Click the small arrow next to the button to choose what you want to edit. This takes you directly to one of the features.

3. Use the Info and Settings tab to edit the description, tags, and other features.

4. Use the Enhancements section to add light, contrast, etc.

5. Click on the Trim button on the Enhancements section to cut any parts of a video if necessary. This might work

if you want to eliminate excess material that might not be professional or attractive.

You can do many other special things within the Edit menu under the Creator Studio section.

Adding Music

You can add background music to your YouTube video. This is great if you need some music in the background. It works better than having a plain video with silence in the background. Here's how to add music:

1. Go to the Music panel on the Edit menu of the Creator Studio.

2. Search for a track to use. You can choose something based on what is popular or on a certain genre.

3. Click any of the music files to find what you feel comfortable with.

4. Select the confirm button on the menu when finished.

YouTube has tens of thousands of music files you can use for the background of your video. These are all ad-free options to use without having to pay anything extra.

You can always use your own music to add onto your video before you upload it. That would require the use of a professional program. You would have to be aware of how the music is made and who owns the rights as you don't want to violate any copyright terms on YouTube.

Fortunately, the music files that YouTube does offer are diverse and come in many forms. They are certified by

YouTube to be free for use. You will not run into any legal problems featuring these music files.

Adding an End Screen

The next thing to decide on is an end screen. This feature of YouTube appears during the final few seconds of a video. It lets you highlight other videos you want to direct people toward. Use this to get people to see other videos relating to something your business offers. Only choose appropriate videos that are relevant to the original one. This is so people see something related to their interests. Your content also has to be compelling enough for someone to click one of the videos you are promoting.

You can insert many things onto your end screen. You can add some thumbnails that link up to other videos on your YouTube channel, a link to a website, or a call-to-action to get people to subscribe to your channel.

To prepare the right end screen features:

1. Go to the End Screen section of the Video Creator Studio editor on the video of your choosing.

Your video must be at least 25 seconds in length to be able to add an end screen.

2. Go to the proper section of the video where you want to add an end screen.

You can only add the end screen during the final 20 seconds of your video.

3. Click the Add Element option.

4. Select the specific item you want to add.

You can add a link to a website provided you have one that has been properly approved. You could also add a link to promote subscriptions to your channel or a link to another video or playlist.

5. Drag the individual items that you have added as desired.

You can move them around various parts of the screen. But watch what is on your video at the end, so you don't add these things in the wrong spots.

The end screen is great for marketing as it draws in more subscribers and lets people know that you have more to share. Use this if you have a lot of videos you want to show or you simply want to obtain some extra subscribers. Whatever your goal, you will find it easy for you to get people to your spot when the end screen is created properly.

Can You Add Annotations?

There is an Annotations listing on the Creator Studio menu, but it is not something you can use. Annotations were offered by YouTube, but they are no longer included as they cannot be read on mobile devices. Many people on YouTube preferred to disable annotations on their videos.

These features were boxes that could be added onto a video. These boxes included additional bits of information relating to something being posted. Anyone could use an annotation to add notes about what is on the screen. Fortunately, a person can easily use the end screen feature to give the same messages.

Do not be surprised if you notice annotations on older videos when comparing what your competitors might be using. Existing annotations on videos that were created before

YouTube did away with them will still appear. However, they can no longer be edited.

If anything, the end screen is more convenient. It is not intrusive and distraction- free. It also offers better space for things to say and actual links that might be more valuable.

Add Cards

Adding cards allows you to ask people to send feedback about your videos among other things. A card is something that appears at any point in a video and invites people to interact. Here are some steps for producing such a card:

1. Go to the Creator Studio and then to the Card section on the space you want to edit.

2. Select Add Card from one of various cards.

You can add a poll, a card promoting your channel, a donation card for nonprofit fundraising, or a link card that goes to your website. Any of these can work if the content you have is valuable and useful.

3. Enter the details. These include a link you want people to visit, a donation button, or a poll. The screen will produce a proper interface for any of these.

4. Choose where you want to place the card. You will have a bit of freedom as to where the card can go.

Getting your videos on YouTube up and running is easy to do when the right plans are made. YouTube has laid out everything you need right through its website. You can use all the resources YouTube provides to help you make the most in marketing your business. Best of all, much of what is offered is free to use. All you need now is a camera to record your videos. You could use editing tools on your own as well, but that's another story.

Chapter 17 – Making the Most of YouTube

YouTube is brilliant for social media campaigns if you know how to use it. You have to make your videos appealing while also stand out. More importantly, you have to produce things that make your promotional channel more intriguing. This will bring in more subscribers and more visits to your site or store. There are a few special tricks for getting your YouTube videos to be easier to read and more dynamic.

Get Verified

You need to be verified to get more out of YouTube. A verified account will have access to more functions. These include the ability to add custom thumbnails to a video or to make your videos a little longer. Authentication ensures that you can do more because YouTube knows that your channel is legitimate. That is, an automated program does not run the channel.

Your account will be listed on YouTube as being fully confirmed. People who go onto your channel will note that it has been certified as a verified channel. People are more likely to trust your channel if they know it has been verified. This is similar to what happens when your Facebook page has been verified.

The process to get verified on YouTube:

1. Go to Youtube.com/verify after you log into your account.

2. Select the country where your channel is based.

3. Choose to get a verification code sent to your mobile phone.

The code can be sent through a text or through an automated voice message. It may take a few minutes for you to get the code sent to your phone.

4. Enter the code.

5. Your account should now be verified.

Using Your Own Custom Thumbnails

When you start using YouTube, you will have the option to work with random thumbnails on each video. Over time, you can be approved to work with custom thumbnails. These add a unique image that lets people see what you want to share before clicking on it. It could include details on what a video is about or some other display feature that is more intriguing to the reader.

You can only get a custom thumbnail added if you are verified on YouTube. You can also use one if you have access to the live streaming system.

To make a custom thumbnail ready:

1. Go to the Video Manager section of your Creator Studio.

2. Click the Edit button on the video you wish to edit.

3. Click the Custom Thumbnail button.

4. Upload a thumbnail you have already produced on your computer.

5. Click to save changes.

The custom thumbnail should be designed so that it draws the user's attention.

What Can a Custom Thumbnail Include?

A custom thumbnail must entail the following:

- The thumbnail can include text or logo features that describe what is on your video. This might produce a more professional appearance to your video.

- You could also choose a specific shot on your video that was not covered by the thumbnails YouTube has automatically generated. Still, this might not be as professional as getting a custom image applied.

- Produce something with a resolution of 1280x720.

- The thumbnail must be 2 MB or less in size.

- A 16:9 aspect ratio is best, as that is the layout used on most devices and players.

Whatever the case may be, make sure the thumbnail is suitable. Like with the actual video itself, your thumbnail is subject to YouTube's content advisory rules. You cannot use something objectionable or questionable for your thumbnail. Be sure it is appropriate and is easy to follow.

Creating a Channel Trailer

A channel trailer is a video that you upload that will be played on your channel page when someone who has not subscribed to your page comes across it. The video usually plays back automatically. The trailer can be any kind of video, but it is best to use one that illustrates what your business is all about. The video is generally the first thing that you should show to someone who is not familiar with your business. It creates a welcome approach to explain to the viewer what you do and what makes your work special.

When a person subscribes to your page, that channel trailer will no longer appear. The channel will just look like any other YouTube page with the newest videos at the front and sections for individual playlists organized. However, the trailer itself is necessary for getting people to become subscribers. Your trailer will make your work interesting and valuable without being unusual in its appearance.

To create a channel trailer:

1. Upload the video that you want to use as your trailer.

2. Go to the Customize Channel button on your channel page after you have logged in.

3. Click on the For New Visitors tab.

There should be two tabs on your channel. The first shows what subscribers to your channel will see. The second is for new visitors.

4. Click on the Channel Trailer box.

5. Select the specific video that will go into the box.

At this point, the trailer will appear on the screen for anyone who has not subscribed to your channel. The video will play automatically after the person gets onto the channel.

What Should the Channel Trailer Include?

The channel trailer can be anything you want it to be. Here are a few of the things to look into when getting a trailer prepared:

- Produce something that explains to people what you do.

- Explain something of value to the viewer. This might include a specific product or service that you want to market.

- Do not keep the trailer too long. Keep it 30 to 60 seconds in length if possible.

- Produce a strong hook in the first few seconds that will get people to pay attention. It might include a question about an issue.

- Make the video as though the viewer has never actually heard of you. The trailer should be an introduction.

- Ask people to subscribe to your channel.

Creating Playlists

Maybe you've got some YouTube videos that link up to each other in some way. For instance, you might run a website that offers hosting services. Perhaps you have some videos that show how to work with a blogging platform. Maybe you have a series of videos about online commerce functions and how a web host handles them. Whatever the case is, you could potentially have some videos that link up to each other based on the content or subject matter.

You can create playlists highlighting everything that is similar in some way. With a playlist, you share information in a series of organized spaces that let people know specific things about your business. They might also include points on your business and how it operates, or your knowledge about things relating to your niche.

To create a playlist:

1. Go to a video that you want to use in your playlist. This should be the first video in that planned playlist if possible.

2. Click the Add To button under the video.

3. Click on the Create New Playlist option.

4. Enter the name of that new playlist.

5. Go to other videos on your channel and repeat the same. You should have the option to add the video to the new playlist you just created.

6. Go to the Playlist menu on your channel and select Edit Layout on your new playlist. This lets you adjust the order in which the videos will appear on the playlist. You can delete videos from the Edit Layout menu if needed.

Using Captioning

There might be times when someone wants to see your YouTube video, but that person has to keep the sound down to keep from bothering people. Other users might be deaf or hard of hearing. Use captions on your video to bring in more people. A person could click on the proper captioning icon on your video, and a series of captions will appear at the right moment.

Even better, this might help with getting people to find your video. The transcript you use can be loaded up by anyone who watches it. This transcript will be read in a search, thus allowing your video to be easily found when a proper keyword is used. This means your script will make a real difference when trying to get people see your work.

To get captions added to your video:

1. Click the video you want to edit within the Creator Studio.

2. Go to the Subtitles/CC tab.

3. Select the language of the video.

4. Select the method to add your subtitles or captions.

You have the option to let YouTube transcribe your video. This option is not recommended. YouTube's speech recognition algorithm can only go so far when finding out what you are working with. The best method is to create new subtitles yourself.

5. Type something you want to add. Whatever you enter will first appear on the screen at the precise time you entered it.

6. Click the plus button to add the caption.

Try to caption about five to ten seconds of text at a time.

7. Move to the next section of the video where you want a new caption to appear.

8. Enter the next caption.

9. Repeat for the length of the video.

This process takes a bit of effort, but it makes your videos easier for people to understand. It may especially do well for your search engine optimization as you get more keywords from your transcript. This adds to the potential to get a better link for your video.

The video captioning highlights keywords. Clearly, you need to write the script before you produce your video. With captioning, you can at least ensure you are getting the keywords you want emphasized. This should produce a more attractive video with enough valuable data.

Add Calls to Action

You need plenty of calls to action around your YouTube page and your videos. These include calls to encourage people to visit your website or your place of business. More importantly, you have to add calls to action for things relating specifically to YouTube. Interacting with your viewers through your videos and other features is fundamental.

There are a few things you can do when adding calls to action:

- Include a message to tell people in a video to subscribe to your channel.

- Ask people to leave comments in your video. Tell them to let you know what they think about your work.

- Invite people to share your video on other social media sites. Encourage them to use the forwarding features below the video player to.

- Use a link to another site for embedding purposes.

Whatever you do, never appear as if you are forcing or threatening people to do it. Be polite with your calls to action. Invite people to follow you. Do not use aggressive language when asking people to follow your instructions. Your viewers appreciate when you show a sense of control and interest in others on your site.

Chapter 18 – Live Streaming on YouTube

Like Facebook, YouTube offers live streaming functions. This allows you to display things in real time to anyone around the world. It offers a fun layout where you can highlight anything unique or of value to you.

Over the years YouTube has been used to stream various events live. It has streamed concerts, governmental meetings, conferences, sporting events, and much more. The audiences for these events can be impressive as well. For instance, in 2012 nearly eight million people went on YouTube to watch Felix Baumgartner jump out of an aircraft more than 20 miles above the earth's surface.

Fortunately, you don't have to be like Baumgartner and jump from the edge of the planet's atmosphere just to be noticed on YouTube. You just have to produce a smart video conference or other event to interact with people and share anything you want with them.

Live streaming works best when you want to talk with potential customers or wish to go to some special event, and share it online. Several steps must be used when getting a live stream ready.

Use the Stream Now Option

You can start streaming live by using the Stream Now option on your YouTube account. This works when you have an appropriate encoder. The Stream Now selector lets you get onto a streaming session on YouTube right away. Use this to send content at any time; YouTube will automatically start a stream when you get ready and end it when you finish.

1. Go to the Creator Studio and then the Live Streaming section.

2. Set up your encoder.

An encoder is a device or software program that compresses your audio and video into a setup that YouTube can support. You can download one of various encoders for your use including Webcam, Mobile Live, AirServer, SlingStudio, and Gameshow, among many others.

3. Enter a title and description for the video.

4. Add a thumbnail to your stream. This will let people know what your stream is about.

5. Prepare a schedule for when the stream begins. It is recommended to let people know when you will stream ahead of time.

6. Set your privacy setting.

You can make your live stream public or unlisted. Or a private session only available to subscribers, or people who enter with a password. If you wish to make it private, you will be prompted to enter a password for access or to use an option to let subscribers in.

7. Choose the latency option. High-quality latency is the best viewing quality; low-quality latency is best for real-time use.

8. If you only have the rights to the live content, click on the box to archive your stream as unlisted when finished.

Using the Events Option

You can also stream on YouTube through the Events option. The Events choice lets you plan your YouTube stream as a special occasion ahead of time.

1. Go to the Live Streaming section of the Creator Studio.

2. Click the Events section and then the New Live Event option.

3. Enter the basic points of the event.

The critical features to list include the title and description of the event, when it starts and ends, plus any tags you want to incorporate.

4. Set the privacy option. Use Public for events that appear on your channel.

5. Select the Quick option. This will get the event supported through YouTube Live, the official live streaming support system used by YouTube.

6. Make sure the item you use for recording yourself is accessible during the event.

Using Live Chat

The Live Chat feature on YouTube lets you interact with others during a live streaming event. This lets you talk to people online about anything happening in your stream.

The chat box appears on the right-hand side of your video player. It is visible when the video recording process is running.

How to use Live Chat:

1. Use either the Top chat or Live chat display. The Top chat option filters out possible spam messages. The Live chat displays everything.

2. Assign a moderator for your chat. Click on the three dots near your chat box and enter someone's username to be approved as a moderator.

Make sure the moderator is also someone within your business. The moderator will review all the things being entered into a live chat. The person should let you know what people are saying.

3. Go to the Community Settings section of the live chat and enter blocked words. Any chat messages that feature certain words will be blocked.

4. Block viewers from your live chat if they become abusive by clicking next to a questionable chat message, going to the writer's YouTube channel, and then clicking on the Block flag from the user's About page.

All the comments left during your chat will be accessible under your live streaming player after the stream ends.

Using Live Metrics

Make sure you read the live analytics or metrics on your streaming video. This gives you information on how many people are watching, how many messages are coming into your video, and how long people have been viewing your video and some other points.

You will not have access to every metric while you are recording. Use the YouTube Analytics feature to identify how your videos are working a few days after the stream ends. Additional details can be found in the YouTube Analytics chapter.

Tips for Live Streaming

There are a few important tips when getting your live streaming experience on YouTube to work for you:

- Let people on YouTube know about your live stream as soon as possible. Tell them when you will stream so they can plan to get onto your page at a certain time.

- Keep a recorded archive of your live event on your hard drive if possible. This ensures you can get the event uploaded onto your page later on.

- Keep the stream looking professional. Use a high-quality camera and microphone to make your stream look its finest. Try to keep the microphone from being visible on the camera; a camera with a built-in microphone might be best.

- You have the option to use a webcam for streaming if needed. A webcam can work to get something ready for recording without having to use an encoder. Make sure the webcam is compatible with YouTube and that It's of good quality.

- Respond to comments during your live stream if possible. Address those who comment by name so people will see that you listen to them and that you have a vested interested in what they say.

- You can always record a live stream while on the go. Make sure the camera and microphone are steady so people can hear and see you properly.

A live stream on YouTube is fun because it offers a unique way to interact with people. Try this option to make your business visible on YouTube. Plan, so you have the best possible event ready.

Chapter 19 – Using Paid Ads on YouTube Through Google AdWords

The next point for using YouTube for your social media marketing is to utilize the paid ads feature on the site. The TrueView ad system lets you reach people who want to watch your videos on YouTube. Much of this is thanks to how YouTube works with the Google AdWords system.

Google AdWords is a method that lets people get their advertisements to appear higher up on a search. When a person's link is connected to a specific keyword, that link will appear at the top of a search page for that word. Since Google controls YouTube, it should not be difficult to use the marketing system offered here.

For YouTube, AdWords works a little differently. You will spend money on each click someone puts onto your video or every time someone watches your video. The videos and ads you produce will be displayed based on the keywords someone uses to search or the audience you target. The amount you spend depends on how many people click on your ad. A budget can also be set up so that your ad will be removed after you have spent a specified amount.

How Will Your Ad Be Displayed?

There are three ways your ad can be displayed on YouTube through AdWords:

1. It appears as a video that shows up before the desired video.

You can get your ad to play before someone's expected video comes up on YouTube. The user has the option to skip the ad after the first five seconds. You will only have to pay for the video ad when someone watches at least 30 seconds of it. An ad promoting the video will also appear on the top-right corner of the screen after the user watches or skips the video. The skip option makes it all the more important for you to draw the viewer's attention during the first few seconds of the ad.

2. It could also show up on another website.

Your video might appear on an outside website through an embedded player. Provided the video is similar in focus to the content on that site. You will pay for the ad when someone watches enough of the video.

3. It can appear on a YouTube search.

As with AdWords on Google, AdWords on YouTube will have your video appear at the top of a search listing. This is when the keyword someone searches for matches up with yours. You will pay money when someone clicks on the link.

Steps to Follow

1. Set up a Google AdWords account at adwords.google.com.

You will have to enter your contact information while also offer details on how you will pay for your ads.

2. Go to the Campaigns tab and then click on the +Campaign option.

3. Select the ad you want to work with. Enter the title of your ad, and the proper one should be displayed.

4. Enter the headline you wish to use.

5. Write a few lines describing the ad.

6. Determine where the ad will send people.

You can get the ad to redirect people to either your YouTube channel or your home page.

7. Choose the thumbnail you wish to display.

8. Determine the total amount of money you will spend on the ad. This includes how much you will spend for each click and the maximum budget.

The campaign will continue as long as it needs to. You can always remove your ad from the AdWords system on your own later if needed. Don't forget to include a proper payment system for how you will pay for the ads.

You can use a daily budget followed by the maximum cost-per-view. For instance, you could spend up to $0.05 per view for a $10 daily budget. This means your video can appear all day long until 200 people click or watch it and give you qualifying views. The total will reset the next day.

9. Determine the audience that your video will target.

Your target audience could be based on:

- Geographic location

- Age

- Gender

- Keyword interests

Make sure you enter the proper parameters based on the video you are promoting. Be specific if you have a particular need for marketing. Remember, your possible reach will shrink when you are more specific. The cost per click or view might also change depending on where you go.

Key Tips

- Always use proper keywords in your video's description.

- Keep the title appealing and friendly so that the user will want to see the ad.

- The content of your video should be relevant to whatever keywords you are incorporating into it.

- Get the viewer's attention as soon as possible. Get it in the first five seconds so the viewer will not skip your ad.

- Be free to tell a longer story if desired. Your video ad can last a few minutes if you want it to.

- Give viewers information on how to act at the end. Ask them to click on a link to your site or to subscribe to your channel.

- Use an end screen during the final ten seconds. The screen should tell the viewer what action to take.

- Be specific when entering in the demographics for your ad. Think about who might be interested in your business when getting this data entered.

What About Bumper Ads?

You can use bumper ads on YouTube if you prefer as well. A bumper ad is a six-second message that lets you create some buzz over what you have. It is not an ad that people can skip either; then again, it is a short commercial. You would have to create a new short ad that can be utilized as a bumper to make this option work.

1. Go to the Campaigns tab of your AdWords account and select the video you want to use. Make sure the ad is short enough to be a bumper.

2. Go to the Video Ad Formats section and select the Bumper option.

3. Prepare your budget.

4. Choose where you want to market your ads at.

5. Save your advertisement.

Prepare a unique and convenient six-second ad to make your bumper spot attractive and visible. It should be designed with a look that is interesting and special in some way. After all, you only have a limited amount of time to make it attractive.

Creating Ad Groups

Ad groups let you link several video advertisements together. The ads can work with the same budget and target the same people. You can get one ad group to target a specific audience while a second group focuses on a different grouping.

The steps for getting ad groups ready are as follows:

1. Go to the Campaigns section and click on the Ad Groups tab.

2. Enter a name for the ad group.

3. Enter the specific videos you want to use in the ad group.

4. Choose whether the ads will be ones listed on YouTube searches or in-stream ads that play before videos. You can only use one ad format at a time.

5. Enter the bid amount and budgeting information you wish to use plus the targeting options.

6. Save the ad group.

Your ad groups can be diverse and organized in many forms. You can produce one ad group that introduces people to your business. Another could feature videos that are for people who are already familiar with your brand. Keeping separate groups ready ensures you will establish ads that target different groups of people. You need to use different campaigns with multiple ad groups that work for everyone- ones who know who you are, those who want to know more, and the people who have no idea who you are.

Chapter 20 – Using YouTube Analytics

YouTube has a popular analytics tool you can use to identify how well people are accessing your videos. Use this to identify how people are responding to your videos and who is watching them. This lets you tailor your ad campaign toward those who watch your work. Use this part of YouTube to understand how well your videos are working and how to make them more visible and efficient.

To make YouTube Analytics work for you:

1. Go to the Creator Studio.

2. Click on the Analytics tab.

This should list information on everything in your channel based on:

- How many views of your videos within a certain time period.

- How long people watched those videos.

- The average duration of each view.

- How many people liked or disliked your videos.

- How many shares, comments, or new subscribers you attracted.

- The top ten videos on your site based on various factors.

- Geographic information on who watches your videos.

- Traffic sources related to how and where people access a video.

- Demographic information about who uses your video.

3. Click on any of the sections of the Analytics page. Doing so lets you review more specifics about who watches your channel, how long people watch it for, and so forth.

4. Click on a specific video name on any section in your analytics reports.

This will take you to the analytics for that one specific video.

5. Use the sections on the left-hand side to identify all the specifics relating to the video you have chosen.

This lets you see how well certain videos are working. YouTube offers analytical information on every video.

6. Click on the date search at the top-right part of the screen to change the range of dates that the Analytics menu will display information.

You can review information based on what happened in the past week, month, year, or any custom range you want.

The data you get from YouTube's Analytics feature will help you identify everything happening on your site. Use it consistently to understand which ads are working the best for your YouTube marketing.

Chapter 21 –Instagram

In addition to writing on Facebook or sharing videos on YouTube, you can also use images in your social media marketing campaign. Thanks to Instagram; one of the hottest spots in the social media world. What is Instagram and how can you use it for your social media marketing demands?

About Instagram

Instagram was created in 2010 originally as an app for the iOS operating system on Apple devices. A few years later, it was introduced for Android and Windows Mobile devices.

The general concept of Instagram was to let people take photos with their mobile devices and share them on a social media network. Moreover, you can do other things than just send photos; post messages along with the photos and add some fun digital filters.

The Instagram program became a popular place for marketing, but it is also became very popular thanks in part to its tie to Facebook. In 2012, Facebook acquired Instagram for $1 billion. Today it is estimated that Instagram has around 375 million users around the world. Over the years, around 40 billion photos have been uploaded to Instagram. That is how powerful and viable Instagram is. The fact that it has full backing from Facebook makes Instagram even more popular.

Who Uses Instagram?

Instagram became a popular place to many people over the years. In 2017 Sprout Social collected the following information about Instagram:

- A majority of people on Instagram are in the 18-29 age range.

- Most of the people on Instagram are in urban environments.

- While around 26% of men online use Instagram, nearly 38% of women use it.

- There are no real disparities between Instagram users regarding income. People making $75,000 annually or more use Instagram, as those who earn less than $30,000 a year.

The statistics show that today's younger generation is more interested in Instagram than other social media platforms. This suggests that targeting younger people on Instagram is a good idea. If anything, a glance at the popular accounts on Instagram should prove it is an ideal place to visit when targeting younger audiences.

Some of the favorite accounts on Instagram include the world's hottest celebrities. It is projected that musician and actress Selena Gomez beats them all with more than 130 million followers Instagram followers. Fellow music stars Beyonce and Taylor Swift are also huge names as well as professional soccer stars Cristiano Ronaldo, Lionel Messi, and Neymar.

Businesses can get many followers on Instagram too. The prominent magazine National Geographic has more than 80 million followers. The shoe and sportswear company Nike has around 75 million followers. The Real Madrid and FC Barcelona soccer teams are also immensely popular on Instagram.

It confirms that Instagram is a viable and appealing option on social media. With so many viewers on Instagram, you are bound to find plenty of interest in your work. Who knows, maybe someday Selena Gomez or Cristiano Ronaldo will see something on your site that is fascinating and mention your work to their tens of millions of followers?

What You Can Do With Instagram

You can use Instagram to promote anything your business offers. You can post pictures or short videos of what you sell. Media relating to your line of work can be posted and shared. You can even include striking images of some of the places where your products could be used. There are no limits as to what you can do with your Instagram campaign.

Like any other social media site, you can interact with others on Instagram. You can leave comments on other videos and tag them to others who might be interested. Do this with anything relating to your business. Just search through Instagram to find things relating to your interests. You will be impressed at how assorted and vast Instagram is. With the site growing as well as it has been, it only makes sense to promote your business there.

An Important Note

Although Instagram is useful, you can only upload photos and videos onto your account through a mobile device. Instagram does not support desktop uploads. This means all the photos used for your Instagram account need to be taken by a Smartphone or tablet. Make sure the device you have is of good quality, so it is easier to take photos and share them in a professional manner.

You also have the option to upload any photos or videos onto a phone, so you can upload them onto Instagram. Instagram's overall layout might make some photos look a little different. You can use the editing features that Instagram comes with, but the edits might not be as thorough as what a traditional desktop program offers.

Chapter 22 – Using Instagram Correctly

Instagram offers a special setup where you can quickly get photos and videos added to your page. It lets you upload them from your mobile device into your account. It is a simplified approach to handle your content by letting you upload files from the camera feature on your mobile device. This chapter is about helping you make the most of your photos and videos to market your business.

Use a Business Profile

You need an Instagram Business Profile to get the service to work for you. With this, you can gain access to many functions including advertising features and analytical insights. Best of all, it is easy to get your profile set up for business functions. You only need to get a Facebook account ready to help:

1. Click the circular settings icon on your profile page.

2. Tap the option to switch your profile to a business one.

3. Choose the Facebook page that you will link to your Instagram profile.

4. Keep your account set to public.

5. Check your business' contact information. Make sure the content is accurate before you confirm it.

This lets your Instagram channel become a business page devoted exclusively to what you offer. Your page will display not only the videos and photos you add but also contains important details related to your business. This includes information on your location and ways of communication. The business layout even lets the user click a Contact button. This button allows a person to call or email you or to get directions making it easier for people to reach you.

Properly Edit Your Photos

Now that you have a business-oriented Instagram account, you need to add content. It is one thing to add photos and videos to the account, but it is even more important that the subject matter is good. This is to establish a professional look on your page. Your marketing campaign will run smoothly if you edit your photos fittingly. Here are a few things to do:

1. Consider uploading a photo you have put on your mobile device from another source.

You have the options to take a photo and send it immediately to Instagram or to upload a photo that you have taken elsewhere. This could be great for professional photos taken a while ago that you might want to share on Instagram. Your photo can be properly edited to look clear and useful.

You could also upload a photo that you have taken on your device. Instagram's app supports all major mobile devices. Any device that can use the Instagram app can link to its camera feature.

2. After you upload a photo, click on the photo's triple dot emblem.

3. Click on the Edit option.

4. Go to the Adjust menu.

This gives you access to effects and filters you can utilize. You have the option to add many unique physical features to add an outstanding look to your photo. The next few steps involve some of these special filters.

5. Use the Crop option to move the photo or to zoom in so only a certain bit of that photo will appear on the screen.

This is ideal if you have a photo that might be too large for Instagram to display or if you want to focus on one specific aspect of the photo.

6. Use the Straighten option to adjust how the photo looks. This entails tilting the video to the left or right, so everything looks level.

This is critical if your photo appears to have been taken from an angle. An image will look more professional if the photo is upright.

7. Click the circle icon to switch your photo from a portrait orientation to a landscape option. You can use this to see if a photo looks best on one format versus the other.

8. Add a border by clicking on the square-shaped icon.

Working With a Video

You can add videos to your Instagram page. Videos can be up to 60 seconds in length. This should be sufficient to highlight a product demonstration or a brief interview. When getting a video ready, recognize what you will get from it and how it can be displayed on anyone's mobile device. There are a few points to follow for a video on Instagram working for your business:

1. Rather than just taking a video on the fly, upload a video from your mobile device's library.

Although you have the option to record a video and get it uploaded onto Instagram right away, it might be best to use a video you already uploaded onto your page. Anything that has been edited and prepared for use is always perfect. Upload that video to your mobile device, which can then upload the file to Instagram.

2. Use the Trim option to cut parts out of videos.

With the Trim feature, you can choose to cut out bits of a video or even add other video files onto an existing upload. This is great if you want to keep a video streamlined.

3. Click on the Write a Caption option to add a caption.

A caption lets people read what you say on a video. After you make your video, you can enter a caption that matches it. You have the option to edit or add something later on via the account page.

Anything over 60-seconds is cut from your video. Keep everything timed so you don't go beyond that mark. Avoid dividing larger videos into smaller Instagram posts; that would be inconvenient, not to mention most people might not look at many smaller videos in a row.

Add a Location

One idea for Instagram marketing involves adding a location to your photos or videos. A location listing includes information on where a photo or video was taken. It could also be edited to display where your business is based. This lets you reach local users as they search for certain keywords on Instagram, who get responses from their local communities first. This means you might appear first on a search page or at least close to it depending on where the person is located.

1. Upload or shoot a photo or video.

2. Go to the Add Location option after adding your effects and filters.

3. Search for your location and enter it.

4. Click on the Share button.

The information can be edited on your post through your Instagram account.

Working with Facebook Locations

Instagram allows you to use a Facebook location for your photos or videos. This is ideal if you are trying to enter a particular spot, but it does not exist on Instagram.

1. Log into your Facebook account through the mobile device you use to access Instagram.

2. Make sure you have the Check-In feature on your account. It lists where your business is located.

3. After the location has been confirmed and added to Facebook, you can add your location to your Instagram account. Use the steps listed for a general location and incorporate them.

Refer to the Facebook chapters for details on how the Check-In feature works.

Linking With Facebook

Getting your Instagram account connected to Facebook is a valuable idea. You can get your Instagram account linked to share your posts on Facebook. Since Facebook's pages are optimized to support Instagram posts, there are no worries about your Instagram shots looking odd on your Facebook feed. Use these steps to connect your account to Facebook.

1. Tap the three dot icon on your Instagram profile.

2. Scroll to the Linked Accounts option.

3. Enter the Facebook option.

4. Add your login information for your business' Facebook account.

5. Do this for as many Instagram accounts as you need. You can get multiple accounts linked to a single Facebook page.

6. Go to your Facebook page to adjust how the photos are viewed. To begin, only friends on your page will see the photos. Change the settings to make your photos available to everyone.

7. You can also use the same menu to separate the Facebook account from your Instagram account.

Instagram has similar features to share your work with others on Tumblr and Twitter as well. It is best to use this for Facebook in the early stages because Facebook and Instagram closely linked to one another. Instagram's layout works great on Facebook.

What About Stories?

Stories can be used on your Instagram account as well. A story is a photo of something you want to share for a brief period. A story photo will stay online for 24 hours before it is removed. This is appealing to promote live events or activities, but not for when you need something longer lasting. Only use Stories on Instagram if you want to post brief updates on what you are doing right now and do not plan on saving for later use.

Chapter 23 – Marketing on Instagram

Statist claims that as of late 2017, there are around 800 million people around the world using Instagram. They also remark that nearly a million different groups are advertising on Instagram at any given time. This proves Instagram is a valuable and useful option for your marketing. Instagram does not have its own dedicated advertising management system. Rather, you use the Facebook Ads Manager to get manage your ads.

You already learned about Ads Manager earlier in this guide. Make sure you have a suitable Facebook account so it works for you.

The process entails getting your Instagram ads to appear prominently.

Getting Your Instagram Ads Supported Through Facebook

Be certain that your Facebook account is properly linked to your Instagram account before you start this process.

1. Go to the Facebook Ads Manager.

2. Set the objective you have for your campaign.

3. Enter your target audience. This is who will be more likely to see the ad.

4. When choosing your placements, go to the Instagram section under the Platforms tab.

5. Click to have your Instagram feed work as an ad system.

6. Set up a budget and timing schedule for your campaign.

7. Create your Instagram ad.

This leads to the next process.

Creating an Instagram Ad

Follow these steps to create your own Instagram ad to display on the platform:

1. Choose the type of ad.

You can utilize one of these options:

- An image feed ad displays an image that you have posted. This is great for most intentions.

- An image story ad is similar to an image feed but for stories.

- A video feed ad helps you post a video online.

- A carousel feed ad links many images together in a layout to scroll through. You can choose where individual images go on the carousel as is on Facebook.

2. Select a photo, video, or series of photos from your Instagram account.

3. Review the description, hashtags, and other features displayed next to the photo.

4. Confirm that you will use the photo or other bits of media on your Instagram ads.

5. Add a call-to-action button on the photo at the end. The program will let you choose from ya variet buttons for subscribing to a page, downloading an app, going to a website, and so forth.

The Ads Manager will receive your Instagram posts and make them available for audiences on Facebook and Instagram.

What Is the Cost Per Click?

The cost per click for Instagram ads can be pricey. It can be between 50 to 80 cents per click. Some ads might cost a few dollars per click if they are for very popular keywords or certain subjects. Fortunately, you can always organize the budget on your campaign to keep it reasonable. The demand for something of interest and the potential reach will influence the total cost per click. Be aware of this when setting your marketing plans.

Promote Posts

There is also the option to promote individual posts on your account. By promoting a post, that photo or video appears first on a search for words relating to that post. It will appear when the keywords in the description are used for a search. This is best when you want to make a popular post more visible.

To promote your post:

1. Make sure your profile is a business one first. Refer to the previous Instagram section of this guide.

2. Tap on the post you want to promote.

3. Click the Promote option under the post.

4. Enter details on the post reach.

5. List your budget based on what you will spend in a 24-hour period and your maximum price per click.

6. Enter how long you want the post to be promoted.

7. Confirm the details and click the Promote button.

It might take an hour or so for your post to be officially promoted. Instagram reviews content to secure it is appropriate.

Important Tips For an Instagram Campaign

As great as your Instagram marketing campaign can be, watch carefully for how your photos and videos are organized. There are a few vital tips to get a campaign to work its best:

- Create a distinct personality in each ad.

- Use proper keywords in your description to make your work easier to reach.

- The content in your photo is relevant to your marketing message.

- Use creative hashtags that lets people share what you are doing. Be specific with your hashtags, but don't forget to use ones relevant to the message.

- Invite people to tag others who might be interested in your Instagram ads. This means people would send the photo to other people on the site.

- Don't be afraid to make some of your posts detailed. While simple posts can be easy to read, some photos with many features can be interesting. People might try to look at all the details of such a shot.

When Should You Post?

It is typically best to post ads on Instagram during the later parts of the day when people are not working. You will easily get your message out when you post during off-work hours. This is due to the immersive layout that Instagram uses. It would be tough for users to see your ads on Instagram if they don't access it at work.

Overall, the process for advertising on Instagram is similar to that of advertising on Facebook. Instagram uses a great visual design you can take advantage of. Watch how you post on Instagram and that you utilize the right images or videos. Make sure you use the precise instructions for uploading too. While it is easy to add a new post from the camera in your mobile device, it is just as easy to upload something onto that device and move it to Instagram.

Chapter 24 – Twitter

Twitter is a social media platform that became a very big deal. Brevity is the key part of Twitter as it focuses on shorter messages. Twitter is trendy for how quickly it can break news. Nor does it take much to share messages. Use this for your social media marketing campaign if you know how to make it work right.

The basic concept of Twitter is simple. With this social media site, you can share content in the form of brief messages, or tweets as they are called, that are only 280 characters long. You can even add small photos or videos onto your messages or tweets.

Twitter has become a noteworthy social media field to enjoy working with. When on Twitter, you will have a limited number of characters to use when sending messages. This is perfect as it lets you be brief and direct.

Twitter has become very popular in today's social media marketing field. You might have read stories about many companies using Twitter in creative ways. They use it to break stories about what they are doing or to interact with people in special ways. Twitter is easy to use and fun to work with, thus making it popular with businesses. Use Twitter today to help get online and show people what your business has to offer.

This place is an established option for social media that people have trusted since 2006. According to Statista, there are around 330 million active users on Twitter every month.

Twitter is always making news based on the individuals who are on it, the things being promoted there, and even changes to how Twitter operates. It was a very big story in late 2017 when Twitter expanded its maximum character total per tweet from 140 to the current 280-character limit.

Why Use Twitter?

Twitter sounds like a simple place, but some businesses might be appalled by it. They might be unimpressed that you can only interact using 280 characters at a time. Others might feel it is too casual. The truth is, Twitter is a viable place for marketing. After all, hundreds of millions of people are using Twitter right now.

There is one reason that stands out above why should you use Twitter – it helps to interact with the public in the simplest way possible.

People want to interact with companies and brands that they are interested in. They want to feel they are appreciated and that their voices and concerns are heard. By using Twitter, you can start conversations with people and talk about anything of interest. Discuss things relating to your brand or products you want to sell among other subjects. You can also respond to messages on Twitter.

Who Uses Twitter?

For the most part Twitter tends to be used by younger audiences. It is big with 18-29-year-olds. Sprout Social asserts that more than a third of all Twitter users are in that age range. Twitter users are rather diverse. Older adults use it, those who have college educations, and those who don't. This makes Twitter even more enticing to use for promoting your products on valuable and useful social media sites.

What Can You Do With Twitter?

What you can do when marketing yourself on Twitter is endless. You can use Twitter to:

- Talk about new products or services.

- Promote special sales and events.

- Interact with people about what you offer.

- Post pictures of the items you sell.

- Resolve disputes or answer questions.

Twitter is all about producing a friendly space for interaction. You will get a little closer to your clients when you use Twitter to converse with them.

The key point is that Twitter is one of the most valuable places to consider when getting your social media campaign up and running. With Twitter, you can quickly get online and share things with others. Discuss anything you want and even start conversations. You will be impressed with how well Twitter works to market your business.

A Quick Note

The information in this chapter focuses primarily on the desktop or laptop version of Twitter. While many of these features can work on a mobile app, it is easier to use the desktop version to take advantage of its marketing capabilities. This does not mean that you should not use a mobile device to make Twitter work for you.

Chapter 25 – Optimizing Your Twitter Account

The first part of Twitter marketing involves getting your Twitter account fully optimized. This produces a great layout that people can identify when they first see your Twitter page. You can even use this to let people know who you are when leaving tweets on other feeds. The image profile and name should be displayed on anything you post. Other details on your profile may also appear when someone moves a mouse cursor over your profile picture.

Get Your Account Ready

Prepare an account or handle that fits your needs.

To get your handle ready:

1. When signing up for Twitter, enter your full name, email address, and password.

2. Enter your mobile number if applicable.

3. Enter your user name. This is the main Twitter handle that identifies you. This can be changed later.

4. List your interests. Choose categories and items that relate to your business.

If you are running a bookstore, click the Arts and Culture option and select Literature. For an auto body shop, click Lifestyle and then go for Car Culture. Entering these specifics helps to make your Twitter posts more relevant to people who share those interests. This allows your Twitter feed to be easy to spot on other feeds.

5. You can choose to select people who have interests similar to yours. You could add credibility to your handle if you have a few people to follow from the start.

Your account should be ready to utilize at this point. Now you can use Twitter to promote your business.

Getting a Good Profile Ready

Get your profile prepared correctly. This is different from your account; your profile displays details about yourself and your line of work. Create a detailed and thorough profile that lists everything relevant to your work.

1. Go to the Edit Profile button on your Twitter page.

2. Enter the name that you will use alongside your Twitter handle.

3. Enter a biography that explains what you or your business does. Your bio can only be 160 characters long.

The bio will be visible your Twitter page and when people hover over your bio photo while reading a tweet somewhere else.

4. Add your location.

Your location can include any major metropolitan area. Enter your own custom data if desired, but it is best to use whatever the closest specific area that Twitter generates. Your tweets will be visible on searches by people located in that area.

5. List your website. This could be the official website of your business if you have one.

6. Click on Theme Color to choose the color of your Twitter page.

You can change the theme to let the colors match up with whatever your business logo or other identifying features have. Whatever you do, avoid using anything that might make your tweets hard to read. Feel free to experiment with many color schemes.

7. Add a profile photo in the circle at the top-left. You can upload any kind of photo. It will appear as a circle. You might need to edit the photo.

Try to use your business logo as your profile photo if possible. Make the photo clear and distinguishable, so people know it's you.

8. Add a header photo to the top. A rectangular photo should be added to let people know what your business is about.

You can always update your header based on any special events going on in your business. Create a good header before uploading it and test it to see that it fits the rectangular layout. You can always change your header every few months to keep things fresh.

Get Verified

One thing you will notice on many Twitter accounts is that they feature little blue checkmarks. This means that an account is verified. A verified Twitter feed is one where the site confirms that a certain person is running a site or business. This is important for gaining trust. People are more likely to trust verified sites than ones that don't have the blue checkmark.

To have your feed verified:

1. Get your profile filled out completely. Enter every detail on the site.

2. Include a verified phone number.

You will have to respond to a text sent to that phone number. Check the number on that text and enter into Twitter to confirm.

3. Enter your email address and verify it.

You should go to your email inbox and click on the email sent by Twitter. Authenticate your identity.

4. List your birthday.

5. List all your tweets as being public. Private tweets that only a few people can view might suggest you are trying to hide something.

6. Use the proper verification form. Twitter should give you this form to confirm your identity after you have completed all these steps.

Twitter will verify your account as soon as possible. You should get a message from Twitter saying that your verification efforts have been confirmed.

Always follow the appropriate rules of conduct on Twitter if you want to remain verified. People who abuse those rules and do not follow them are at risk of having their verification removed. It makes it tougher for people to market their sites.

Your Twitter account should be fully optimized at this point. Use your account to get in touch with anyone directly. The next chapter is about using Twitter to make your work stand out and be of use to more people.

Chapter 26 – Getting the Most Out of Your Tweets

The messages you post on Twitter are vital to your success with the platform. Create thoughtful, unique, and appealing messages for everyone on Twitter to read. A few helpful strategies can be utilized for better chances of getting your tweets read by more people. More importantly, thanks to people being more likely to trust your work and your words, these tweets can lead to extra followers.

Be Creative

It is understood that the best Twitter feeds are the most creative. They can involve funny anecdotes, thoughtful quotes, how-to information, or anything else. Think about what you want to say and stick with it as you produce an attractive Twitter feed. Let the viewers know you have something to share with them and that you're someone they can trust.

Stay with one Particular Style

Think about how you're going to post things on Twitter. Do you want to have a light-hearted approach to tweeting? Would you rather be straightforward and direct with the public? Whatever it is, determine the attitude and style you will follow and stick with it for as long as you can. Be consistent with all of your posts on Twitter.

Do not shift your attitude or style on a whim or else people might be confused. Some might even think your Twitter profile was hacked into.

Stay Transparent

Like with any other social media site, be fully transparent when talking to people on Twitter. Let people know what you are doing and what makes your business important. People appreciate when they hear from you and see how direct you are with them. They will retweet your messages to others as a result, thus adding to your exposure.

Add a Poll

One way to get people to talk on your Twitter feed is to add a poll. This lets people interact with you by voting on something that interests them.

To produce a poll:

1. Enter a question at the top part of your page.

2. Enter a few choices of answers.

3. Click the Add a Choice button for each time you add another choice on your poll.

4. List how long you want the poll to last. The poll will close after that time expires.

5. Click the Tweet button to get your poll out to the public.

With a poll, you can ask people about what are their favorite things about you. Ask about what products they might be interested in. Perhaps you could get your followers' opinion on some new story or trend. Whatever the case is, your poll will help you gauge what people are thinking. This works best if you can get more responses. A counter will display how many people have replied to your poll in real time.

Pin a Tweet

One way to make people on your Twitter page really know what you are up to is by pinning a tweet. This works when you take a previous tweet and post it at the very top of your feed. It will be the first thing people view when they access your

Twitter page. This pinned tweet could be a special promotion or a general message relating to something of value to your potential customers.

To pin a tweet:

1. Click the More option on a tweet you have posted. This is located at the top-right part of the message.

2. Click the option to pin the tweet to the top of your page.

3. The tweet should now be listed as a pinned tweet at the very top.

Make sure the tweet you pin is relevant to your work and is something you really want to promote. Your tweet can be new or old. Just keep the question related to whatever you want to promote.

Be sure to remove the pin from your tweet if you no longer need it or you want to pin something new. You can click on the posted tweet to remove the pin after a while. Just go back to the More option to remove the pin.

You can leave a pinned tweet up as long as you want. It is best to change it every few weeks or months if possible. You need to keep your Twitter page fresh, so people aren't always reading the same things every day. Besides, people will want to see new updates on your pinned tweet to see anything news and what is changing where you are. Look at it carefully to create something valuable for your promotional plans on your main site.

What Should a Pinned Tweet Involve?

A pinned tweet could involve anything. Some tweets are more appropriate for pinning. You can use anything as your pinned tweet, but you should still be cautious when planning such a feature. Your pinned tweet might involve:

- Details on something new your business has to offer.

- A special message to your fans.

- A statement of your business' mission.

- An announcement relating to an upcoming or ongoing event.

- Anything that might be time-sensitive; this could involve a sale or any other limited-run engagement.

Add a Location

Use the location feature when targeting people within a certain area. Enter the location information on a tweet to let people know where you are or where the tweet has originated. The message will appear on searches from people located near the location of the tweet. This is ideal if you want a specific vicinity to see what you are posting. Use this to let people know where to reach you if you are promoting a big event or you want visitors in a certain place in a short time.

To add a location:

1. Click on the location button on the tweet box. You might have to activate the location feature.

2. A location should automatically appear on the box. This should display details on your whereabouts.

3. Click on the location name to specify where you are. You can use a specific neighborhood or city in the listing.

4. Enter the rest of your tweet.

What If You Need More Room?

For most tweets, 280 characters should be good enough. There might be instances when you need more room to explain something. In this case, you should add a secondary tweet to what you are writing. A secondary tweet is one that follows the initial one. It will not appear on the screen until a reader clicks on it. The tweet will become visible below the first one, so the reader can continue with the next tweet. This is perfect if you are trying to explain something extensive and you need extra space to do so.

Here is how to get this secondary tweet ready:

1. Write your first tweet.

2. Click the + icon near the tweet box.

3. Enter the second tweet that will link up to the first one.

4. Do this as often as is needed. When you are finished, click the Tweet All option.

The first tweet in the thread will always be exposed. A user will have to click on that tweet to see the others you have posted. Try to keep the most important bits of information in the first tweet if you can.

Do not use too many tweets at a time. While you could add one or two additional tweets to go under the initial one, use as few of them as possible. Keep everything you write concise. After all, being concise is a part of what Twitter was founded upon.

Retweet or Reply to Relevant Messages

Is somebody on Twitter talking about your business? Maybe someone is discussing something related to your work. Get into the conversation and add your own message or reply. You could even retweet a message that you want to appear on your own feed. These steps will help you get one of these messages onto your page:

1. Go to any other person's tweet.

2. Click the circular arrow button to retweet someone's message. You can add a comment onto the message from there too.

3. Click the caption bubble if you do not wish to retweet a message but you wish to reply to someone. You can leave a full reply to the message. People on your feed will have to click the appropriate tweet to expand it and see the original one you responded to.

Can Pictures Work?

You can always add pictures and short videos to your Twitter posts. You could even add URLs that send people to particular YouTube videos or other pages you might have elsewhere. Twitter can take a URL and convert it to a convenient box that displays where the URL heads. This lets people know what they are doing when on your site. More importantly, it lets people see the contents of the link you are posting. It is useful for building your readers' trust and showing them what you are all about.

Pictures and videos are perfect if you have tweets that you want to use in a paid advertising campaign. You will learn more about that aspect of Twitter later.

If you wish, you could even add GIFs to your Twitter posts. Either upload your own GIF or use one of many GIFs that Twitter has already incorporated into its platform. Just click on the GIF icon and search for something based on the mood or response you wish to convey. This should liven up anything you wish to talk about online.

Using Hashtags Correctly

Hashtags are a huge part of the Twitter culture. With hashtags, people can interact with each other about certain topics,leave responses and notes about the hashtags they see in real time. While hashtags can be appealing and easy to search for, you have to be careful when using them. You can use a few simple strategies when making hashtags on Twitter work for you.

What's Trending?

Consider the trending topics on the right-hand side of your Twitter screen. This lists information about the popular tweets. Some hashtags may be included on these listings. Try to create a new tweet featuring one of the current hashtags.

Make sure the tweet is relevant to your business. Do not tweet a general hashtag; add a few words that connects to what you offer. Show that you have something they might be interested in while relating it to what the prevalent interest is.

A good idea is to change the trends that appear on your screen based on your location or a place you want to target. Select a specific location in your area to get details on what is trending. Sometimes the same hashtags will appear for that region. In other cases, more localized hashtags and trends might appear. You could create relevant content that is with those specific hashtags in that area.

Use Content Hashtags

Not all hashtags are about whatever presently is happening. Use content hashtags to promote your work. A content hashtag is a message that entails something of interest to your work. It relates to what you have to offer. For instance, an auto body shop might use content hashtags such as #mustang, #shelby, #viper, or other things related to what the shop works on.

Such hashtags will make a tweet more visible. Look at the auto body shop example. While searching "mustang," the hashtag "#mustang" will be more likely to appear on their search. This will stand out from other posts showing their work on Ford Mustang vehicles.

Use content hashtags to emphasize whatever your tweets are about. People will have an easier time finding them through a search when you do. Do not use hashtags that have no relation to whatever you are trying to promote. One or two hashtags should be good enough in each post you make.

Review What Others Use

Survey the hashtags others use to determine what to add on your site. See how people who follow your Twitter feed based on the hashtags. You might notice a trend.

Check your competitors to see how they use hashtags. You could use the same hashtags if you wish. However, consider alternatives to those hashtags to create your own dynamic campaign. Look at what is being posted to come up with a good idea of how you will market your business.

Creating Your Own Hashtag

You can always create a personal hashtag for your marketing. By using your individual hashtag, you tell people something interesting about what you are offering. Let a person know about a product or service that is unique or distinct. Think about a few points for getting your special hashtag work to your benefit.

1. Think about what people who visit your Twitter page are interested in.

As mentioned earlier, look at what your subscribers to your feed are saying about your work.

2. Think about the brand image you are representing.

Your hashtag will become a big part of the image you want people to associate with your business and even your Twitter feed. Decide on the words you want to use and how they relate to your image and what your business does.

3. Review any other promotional materials you have.

Your promotional efforts from other places should be explored carefully. Maybe you have a slogan to utilize. Your hashtag could incorporate that slogan.

For instance, the Kit Kat candy bar uses the hashtag #haveabreak quite often. This is relevant to the long-running slogan Kit Kat uses about breaking off individual wafers from a Kit Kat bar. This adds a direct and distinct hashtag that people quickly recognize. It also takes the brand in a new direction. Think about what you can add yourself.

4. Get your message to stand out and be distinctive.

You can do anything to make a hashtag stand out. Use alliteration, for instance. A car repair and maintenance shop might use the hashtag #geargrinder to talk about transmission services, for example.

Whatever you use, think of something that is memorable and stands out. It should be something attractive and one that creates a particular memory in the reader's mind. Look at your signal words and how they relate to your work. Make sure your content is something outstanding and repeated use.

Besides, a business that is closely associated with a certain hashtag might be a little easier for people to depend on.

Think About Signal Words for Regular Events

One way to use Twitter is to hold regular events on your feed. You could hold a special weekly or monthly session where you chat with people about something of interest to them. Maybe promote special seasonal events like sales or product or service rollouts.

You can add signal words into your tweets to make usual events on your feed a big deal. Signal words might incorporate a certain time of day or week. They may also include the specific year an event is held; you can change the year as needed.

Let's say on Wednesdays or Fridays you like to talk about something important in your business. Use a signal word-based hashtags like #wednesdaywit or #fridayfuntime. A monthly chat with your followers could include a basic hashtag relating to the recurring feature. Something like "Monthly Roundup" could utilize a hashtag like #monthlyroundup, for example.

Each hashtag you use should be reviewed to ensure you have a quality message.

Chapter 27 – Paid Advertising on Twitter

You can always promote yourself on Twitter free. By using the right strategies and taking advantage of trends, you can make yourself more visible on Twitter without having to spend a penny. Everything you have read about Twitter so far was about what you can do for marketing free on Twitter.

Sometimes you may need a bit of help get recognized. After all, there are thousands, if not millions, of tweets flying around at any minute of any day. This is where paid advertising can come into play.

Paid advertising is valuable as it helps you make your tweets more visible. You will get your tweets posted on individual pages and pages of other's. In many cases, those posts will be on search pages relating to the subject people are looking for.

You can always use paid advertising to be more visible on Twitter. You can use many helpful options for paid advertising to work for you.

Promoting Tweets

The first form of paid advertising you can use on Twitter is to promote individual tweets. With this option, you can promote any post you have already promoted in some way. This makes your posts visible on more searches.

You might have a tweet that promotes a new product or service you have. You could also have one that announces a massive business event. Or one that includes your business' vision. Some new mantra, or a concept you want to advertise to readers.

1. Make sure your account is approved for promotional purposes.

Your account will be able to promote its tweets if you are active and have been on Twitter for a while. You might have to spend a month or so and be in good standing to be allowed to promote your work.

2. Choose a specific tweet that you want to promote. Make sure it is valuable for promotional needs.

3. Click the Promote This Tweet option on the top-left menu listed on the tweet.

4. Select your target audience.

You can choose to target a specific metropolitan area or country. You also have the option to let your tweet be seen by the whole world. However, keep focused on wherever you want to promote your tweet.

5. Prepare your budget. Review the estimated results for whatever you choose to list. Twitter lets you know the approximate reach based on your marketing budget.

Enter your payment information if you are using this for the first time.

6. Set up the timing for your campaign. List the dates when your tweet will be promoted.

7. Confirm your promotional efforts. The tweet should be promoted for a short time.

This move is perfect if you have a strong-performing tweet that people are responding to. People will be likely to click on and utilize your tweet if they see something that is enticing and unique to them.

Starting an Ad Campaign

The second option you have for paid advertising on Twitter is to use a simple ad campaign. This is where your work is marketed to other people through a special message that is different from your regular feed. It could include a link to your Twitter page or your regular homepage.

Your ad campaign could be utilized to promote your business in general. It could also spotlight a specific aspect of your work. You might have a campaign focusing on just one new product or service. Maybe you opened a new business location and you want to let people know about it. Regardless of the purpose of your campaign, Twitter has made it easy to get your work ready and active.

To plan your Twitter ad campaign:

1. Create the advertisement. Enter the comments and a link. Add a photo or a video; the video will not play unless the user clicks on it.

Make sure you use the right keywords or hashtags. Your ad will be more likely to appear on a search that involves those words or tags.

2. Enter details where your customers are located. Be as specific as possible so Twitter can target your ads to a very particular region.

3. Specify what you are willing to spend each day on your campaign.

Twitter will give you an estimate of what it costs for each time people click on the tweet. It could be a few cents or even a dollar or two.

4. List the days when the campaign will be live.

5. The ad campaign should be ready in a few minutes after you submit your information.

Promoted Account

You could also promote your account in general. With this, your account will be listed in a box on the right-hand side of a screen. It will be listed among many others that might relate to someone's interests. Additionally, a promoted account is great for introducing people to your business if they have not yet seen what you offer.

Think of a promoted account as a type of VIP account. It is one where people will see your name above all else and hopefully be interested in what you highlight. This is exciting and interesting for your business. Show that your work is valuable and distinct in some fashion with a promoted account.

To set up a promoted account:

1. Go to the Twitter Ads page.

2. Check on your handle name, user ID, and profile logo. These are visible on your promoted account listing.

3. Specify you wish to have your account promoted.

4. List where to promote your account. Again, be precise about the locations you where you want to be seen.

5. Set a budget for what you want to spend during each day of your campaign. You will have to pay money for each time someone clicks on your profile name.

Promoted accounts are perfect if you want to drive downloads, app installs, or just increase visits to your Twitter page. You will also make your brand more visible to everyone on Twitter. Having a promoted account might give people a better impression of your business because it stands out among other popular Twitter feeds. This gives you a better approach for marketing your work.

Chapter 28 – Pinterest

Do you want to target people who might be interested in unique products or ideas? Do you have lots of fun photos and images to share with them? If so, Pinterest might be the right social media to market your business.

Pinterest is an attractive social media site that targets creative people. It focuses on images above all else but with some appealing themes. That is, all the content offered on Pinterest illustrates many things of interest including arts and crafts projects.

Pinterest is a social media site that has been in operation since 2010. It displays many pictures relating to fun things people enjoy. It lets people search for and find pictures associated with their interests. As someone clicks on a picture, a full description of that image is listed. A link to a webpage related to that image will also be there.

Pins and Boards

While people can leave comments on Pinterest entries, the best thing to do is to pin them. The bright red Save button on each entry features a pin. When someone clicks on it, that person pins it to one's Pinterest wall. This means that person will save something as an item of interest or motivation. Some users have special buttons on their browsers to pin things they see online even when they aren't on Pinterest.

Boards are important to Pinterest as well. A board is a collection of things on Pinterest. It includes items that relate to a specific topic. A board could be devoted to inspirational quotes. Another could be about traveling to a certain part of the world.

The key point about Pinterest is that it lets people find things they love and share them around the globe. More importantly, it inspires people to do things differently and to be unique. It gets people to ponder about doing things they love. Whether it is visiting new places or trying new recipes, the list is endless and deserves your attention.

What Type of Content on Pinterest?

The content you will find on Pinterest focuses heavily on many aspects relating to culture. When you go on the site, you will find things like:

- Home improvement posts.

- Fashion for women and men.

- Arts and crafts; these include sections for woodworking among others.

- Cooking and recipes.

- Pop culture.

There are no limits to what you can find on Pinterest. Just use the search bar on the top to see what's available.

Who Uses Pinterest?

The Omnicore Agency states that as of January 2018, there are about 175 million active Pinterest users worldwide. Nearly half of them are in the United States. The median age of people who use Pinterest is 40, but more than half of the people on the site are younger. Approximately 50% of the users earn less than $50,000 a year.

An intriguing part of Pinterest is that the majority of people who use the social media site are women, in fact about four-fifths of all people on Pinterest are women. Meanwhile, men make up less than ten percent of the pins on the site. Therefore, Pinterest would be a great place to market yourself if your business focuses on women's needs or concerns.

Chapter 29 – Marketing Ideas on Pinterest

Businesses can use Pinterest for all their marketing endeavors. For instance, a fashion store could use Pinterest to market different outfits they want to sell. It might start its own board or list individual entries on the products it offers. The store could recommend pictures of the many outfits available alongside links to a site where people can buy them. Users could also click on the fashion store's name to reach its individual account or board.

This means Pinterest can make everything you have to offer more exciting and inviting. Are you trying to sell products online? Make Pinterest your own special storefront. Are you looking to offer certain services to people? Post pictures that show all the things your business does. Whatever the case is, your Pinterest account can be utilized to share anything you have. This lets people see what makes your work interesting. Pinterest also inspires people to take action and utilize whatever you market.

Getting a Post Ready

The best thing to do when getting on Pinterest is to produce enough posts relating to your business. This is very easy.

1. Get a Pinterest account.

You can log in with an existing Facebook or Google Plus account if you have one.

2. Go to your account page and select the Create Board option.

3. Enter a name for your board.

4. Click on the plus symbol on the bottom right part of your page.

5. Click the Upload Pin option.

6. Choose a file you want to post onto your page.

7. Enter a title or description for your pin.

8. Enter a source for the content. This source could be your website.

9. Select the board you want to use to add your material. Details on producing your own board will be covered later. Choose a board that is relevant to your subject matter.

Keep the URL as close to the proper page for the image as possible. For instance, a fashion store that is selling a certain dress can use a URL that leads people directly to the part of the shop where the dress is sold.

Edit Your Board

The boards that you post on are the places where people will find what you are highlighting. While they can find your work by searching for it, your board is the place where all your content is included.

To edit your board on Pinterest:

1. Go to your main profile page.

2. Click the pencil-shaped edit button on the board you want to edit.

3. Enter a name for the board related to the subject.

4. Toggle the Secret setting to make the board visible to the public. If the Secret setting is shown, your board will only be visible to people that you have invited to see it.

5. Select an item in the board that you want to use as your cover. You can drag any image to make it visible within the preview box on your cover.

6. Specify the category that the board represents.

7. Enter a description for the board. Make it a description of your website in particular.

This allows you be online and market your work on Pinterest in a unique and valuable way. Check this out when you want to do more with your marketing campaign.

Can You Make Comments?

Don't forget about the commenting features on Pinterest. People can comment on your pins. You can respond to show them that you care about their feedback. You can also comment on other peoples' work. Make sure to you leave comments on spots relevant to your business. Keep your thoughts informative and unique without sounding like a blatant promotion. Your friendly remarks could invite others to visit your individual page to see what you have to offer.

Share Your Work with Other Social Media Sites

The next idea for using Pinterest is to share what you post on the site with other social networking sites. The steps for doing so are simple:

1. Click on the bolt button on your profile page.

2. Go to the Social Networks option.

3. Click to get your account linked to another page.

4. Enter details on your account from one of the pages listed on the site.

5. Click to save settings so the new Pinterest posts can be shared on the selected social media accounts.

Pinterest does not support business-oriented Facebook accounts. Only personal Facebook accounts can work here.

Avoid Calls to Action

Pinterest's user terms state that the site should be a spot where people can peacefully look around and see what is happening. This means people cannot start promoting their work directly. Businesses can buy ads and link their work to their websites or online shops. But they cannot just say things like "Click here to..." or "Act now and..." etc. This is especially important when using actual advertisements.

In short, do not add any direct calls to action on your site as they might be rejected. Instead, talk about things you have made and let people see what they are. The link that you add is a call-to-action in itself. Do not make the things you post sound as if you are desperate for attention.

Chapter 30 – How to Advertise on Pinterest

The next part of working with Pinterest is to know how to advertise on the site. You can use paid advertisements to market your work on Pinterest. Advertising helps you get your individual Pinterest posts to work for you.

Switch to a Business Account

Before you can advertise on Pinterest, you will have to switch your Pinterest feed to a business-oriented one. It is very easy to do this:

1. Go to pinterest.com/business/convert after reaching your account.

2. Enter your business name.

3. List the type of business you are operating.

4. Enter your website if desired.

5. Click the Done button.

Don't forget to enter your payment information when setting up your business account. This is to arrange payment for the ads.

Apply for Promoted Pins

You must also apply for promoted pins on Pinterest. The steps are as follows:

1. Make sure you have a Pinterest business account.

2. Go to ad.pinterest.com.

3. Apply for the promoted pins feature.

4. Wait to be approved; it might take days or even weeks for this to happen.

After you are approved, you will have promoted pins that can be added to individual posts you put up. These pins may be used anywhere on your account.

Getting an Ad Ready

You can purchase ad space on Pinterest as soon as you get a business account with promoted pins:

1. Choose a particular item on your board on which you want to use a promoted pin.

You cannot create new content with the sole intention of using a promoted pin. That pin can only go on something that already exists.

2. Check on the hashtags in your Pinterest post. You can only have one in a promoted post. That hashtag must be relevant to the content.

3. Select a series of keywords that your pin will be linked to. These are words people will use when they conduct a search.

Review the estimated number of weekly impressions you will get out of your work based on the keywords you enter. This is listed at the upper-right part of the screen.

4. Select the people you want to market your work to.

You will be given the option to target people based on location, demographics, and language. You could even set parameters for the specific devices you wish to have your work seen on.

5. List the maximum budget for your campaign.

224

Enter how much you will spend on the campaign during its lifespan. You can let the campaign work for a specific period of time or for as long as needed.

6. Create a campaign.

Each promoted pin you offer should belong to a specific campaign. This can be a series of pins that are related to one another. For instance, a site offering new swimwear could have a campaign featuring pins relating to that type of fashion. You could have a separate campaign that focuses on kids' clothing too.

Make sure the pins are organized in the same campaign. They should work with the same budget and duration. You can use as many campaigns as desired; each should include separate sale offers.

Chapter 31 –Snapchat

Snapchat is an attractive platform that focuses heavily on photography. A few students at Stanford founded Snapchat in 2011. Their idea was to let people share photos in real time. These are not photos that will stay online forever.

The photos that people can share on Snapchat contain Stories. These bits of content appear online for just 24 hours at a time. A single Story can include as many photos as one wants to use. It could include lots of effects and captions too. A photo can be shot on your Smartphone or tablet and then shared with others right away. Each photo is stored on Snapchat's servers for 24 hours before it disappears. It is appropriate that the Snapchat logo features a ghost outline.

Filters and Lenses

A vital part of what makes Snapchat popular is the use of filters and lenses. These features take Snapchat photos and make them more amusing.

Filters can be utilized to create outlines, borders, or other embellishments on a photo. A filter will go over a still image and create an entertaining appearance.

A Lens works with the live camera feature on a Smartphone. By applying a lens, a person can create an amusing image that you can play with on a live camera shot.

These two things can be used to your advantage when using Snapchat. They allow people to have some fun with their camera features. Filters and lenses also let people know more about a business as they will become aware of what that business offers.

An Active Place

Instagram is a popular site used by millions worldwide. Snapchat's official website says that about 180 million people actively use Snapchat throughout the world. The site even claims that active Snapchatters will open the Snapchat app on their devices at least 25 times every day. In addition, they spend at least 30 minutes on Snapchat each day.

How Would You Advertise?

Snapchat focuses its advertising in a distinct campaign. You can buy one of many types of advertisements that appear between pictures on the site. These ads are displayed briefly and will drive people to your website. Programming these ads will bring people to a place where they can buy an app you might be selling.

With Snapchat, you can prepare many things you wish to present online. Check out what Snapchat has to offer, and you will agree it is a strikingly appealing social media site.

Two Important Notes

Snapchat is only available on mobile devices. There are no desktop versions available. Although you can manage some advertising functions on the Snapchat website, you are better off using a mobile device to run everything relating to your campaign.

Some of the ads will lead people directly to your website. The traffic going to your site will always be mobile traffic. Your website needs to be optimized for mobile use. The fact that Snapchat is a mobile-only program makes it possible to quickly get to a website.

Chapter 32 – The Basic Options For Advertising on Snapchat

You can create a Snapchat account and use it to advertise your business. All these advertising options are ones you can afford right now. Other options are available, but as you will see later in this chapter, they are very expensive. They are more than likely too extravagant to use at this time. Those options are essentially for professional companies that have been around for a while and can afford them. This chapter is about what you can use right now.

Start a Campaign

To begin advertising, set up a campaign:

1. Sign up for the Snapchat Ad Manager.

Get an account from the Snapchat website at forbusiness.snapchat.com. It is free to sign up and only takes a few moments.

2. Select the objective.

Your objective could be to get visitors to your site, to have people install your app, or to simply make people aware of your brand.

3. Enter the name of your Snapchat campaign.

4. List when your campaign will start and when it will end.

5. Indicate the maximum amount of money you will spend per day on your campaign.

6. Add the lifetime spending cap for your campaign. This is the maximum budget for the campaign.

7. Select the demographics you wish to reach.

8. Specify the location you want your campaign to target.

9. List the devices to display your campaign .

10. List an amount to spend for every 1,000 impressions your ads get.

Ads You Can Set Up

After getting your campaign ready, choose one of many different ads. Here are some of the top choices:

Snap Ads

Snap ads are the most popular ads on Snapchat. A snap ad is a video ad that appears in between individual Snapchat Stories. The video plays before a user has access to a Story. The video can be skipped after a few seconds. The video will not display between individual shots in the Story.

Use this to market anything your website has to offer. It could even come with a prompt telling people to swipe the screen to reach your website. To make this ad work:

1. Upload a short video you wish to use. The video should be 3 to 10 seconds long.

2. Enter your brand name. This will appear on the top-left of the video.

3. Enter a short headline for the video. It displays next to the brand name.

Long-Form Video

A long-form video is similar to a snap ad but lasts up to ten minutes. Of course, it doesn't have to be that long. The user can choose to skip the ad after a few seconds, thus making it critical to make your point as soon as possible. Create a long-form video when you have something more to say. It might not appear as often as a snap ad, but it provides plenty of exposure if used correctly.

The process for setting this video up almost identical to that of a shorter snap:

1. Upload the video you wish to use.

2. Add the brand name and headline.

3. Add a teaser screen; an image that displays what your video is about.

4. Use a call-to-action at the bottom of the teaser screen. The video begins when the user swipes the bottom of the screen.

Web View

A web view ad directs people to your website. You can use this ad to drive mobile traffic to your page.

1. Create a web view ad that invites people to your page.

2. Upload the content.

3. Produce a link for the ad to direct people.

4. Create a call-to-action button where the user can move quickly to your targeted website.

App Install

An app install works by linking people to a Google Play or App Store page where an app you sell is located. This is particularly for when you have a mobile app.

1. In the Ad Manager, enter details of the mobile app you want people to link to.

2. Prepare an image or short video promoting your app.

3. Add a call-to-action button at the bottom of the picture or video. This will tell people where they to download your work.

A Note for Videos

All videos used for ad purposes on Snapchat must have an H.264 format. It should also support the proper dimensions. In this case, the dimensions are 1,080 pixels wide by 1,920 pixels high. This is an appropriate layout for Smartphones. Check how any video is organized to have more control over how well the video will look when you play it back.

Why Frames or Lenses Might Not Work

You could produce a lens to market your work and make it more interesting. People can access lenses and have fun with them. Thanks to a lens, they could use their front-facing cameras to see themselves and others in a unique way. For instance, the Michael Kors fashion company once had a lens where individuals could see themselves wearing sunglasses from that high-end fashion brand. A Michael Kors emblem appeared on the side to let people know the maker.

While a lens might be appealing, it is probably not going to work for you. Only established businesses afford to set up their own lenses. The price to set up a lens is close to half a million dollars. This is due to the extreme amount of programming needed for a lens plus the potential for massive exposure. In short, a lens isn't necessarily something your business should be aiming to use. Of course, this could all change if your business becomes a huge multi-national corporation.

Frames can be just as expensive too. A frame could create a fun border that you can use to promote your work. But the cost could also be prohibitive; in the thousands of dollars to set up a frame.

Monitoring Your Work

After you produce an Instagram ad and make it live, you can review the ad's performance. The ad performance screen will let you know how your campaigns are working and what is happening with your ads. Use it to review things like:

- How many impressions your ads received.

- How much you spend to get those impressions.

- The number of times people swipe an ad.

This lets you know which ads are more popular. You can even discover how well your campaign runs and if it is as productive as you want it to be.

Chapter 33 –LinkedIn

LinkedIn is different from other platforms where you might market your work. While LinkedIn provides people the opportunity to connect, it is on a more personal level.

LinkedIn is a social media site focused on professional networking. It has more than 500 million users from about 200 countries with around 100 million active users as of 2017. First formed in 2002, the website has been growing ever since. In fact, Microsoft acquired it in 2016. Today it is a trusted space for people looking for career opportunities or establishing strong business relationships.

What Makes LinkedIn Special?

LinkedIn is unlike other social media sites as it concentrates on business functions. It works for employers and employees alike. Individuals use LinkedIn to post information about themselves to businesses and professionals. You can do many things with LinkedIn:

- Post a CV or resume.

- Enter details about one's skills.

- Run a blog focusing on vocation efforts.

- Join groups relating to things one is interested in; these include alumni groups and those associated with companies someone has worked for.

- Find information on new job opportunities.

Businesses can use LinkedIn to market their work and get in touch with people. What a business does with LinkedIn includes:

- Enter background information about the business.

- Catalog job opportunities.

- Create subchannels related to specific functions within the business; these include smaller channels focused on internship programs.

- Post news updates related to the business.

Who Uses LinkedIn?

LinkedIn is a great place if you aim to target professionals. A 2015 Business Insider Intelligence Report disclosed that people who are prosperous and educated use LinkedIn:

- Most of the people who use LinkedIn are at least 35 years old. In fact, the number of LinkedIn users in the 50-64 age grouping is greater than users in the 18-29 age group.

- Close to 40% of all people on LinkedIn have a college degree or greater.

- About 24% of all men who are online have used LinkedIn. Around 19% of women have used it.

- Around one-fifth of all people on LinkedIn earn at least $75,000 a year.

- Close to one-fifth of people on the site earn less than $30,000 a year. Those might be college students who use LinkedIn to access job information and internships, but as the age point proves, older professionals outnumber them.

LinkedIn is an exciting option for your social media marketing because you will reach experienced workers. You will target people who have well-paying jobs and are business-minded. It will do the same for people who want to get into the workplace. This is a very unique marketing option that is beneficial but only if you use it the right way.

Chapter 34 – Using Your Profile to Market Yourself

The first part of using LinkedIn for marketing is to create a profile. This is ideal ot get in touch with people without spending money. Of course, you can invest on ads if you wish, but that is something we will cover in the next chapter.

This chapter focuses on using your profile to get the word out about what you are doing. Depending on how proficient you are, your success in this effort could pay off. You could get in touch with other professionals who might express interest in your work. This could generate several referrals, thus leading to more exposure for your brand. Getting your name out there and establishing strong relationships is what LinkedIn is all about.

Set Up a Profile

Start marketing yourself on LinkedIn with a profile.

After signing up for an account:

1. Post an image of yourself at the top. Use a recent image.

2. Add your business name.

3. List your location. Be very specific about this.

4. Enter your work experience if applicable. Be detailed and write about what you did and when you did it. Keep the data relevant to your current line of work.

5. Include specific skills related to what you are promoting.

Prepare a Company Page

Now get a company page on LinkedIn. You need to have a LinkedIn account and an email address.

1. Add your company's logo in the proper box.

2. Add a cover image at the top of your page. Just like what you use on Twitter, your cover image will be a rectangular banner that displays something of value relating to your business.

3. Go to the About Us section and add a description. This could include a listing of your goals for making your campaign work.

Your company page is what you will use to reach out to people. Your marketing efforts will be more successful if you have a dedicated company page that lists information on all the things you offer.

Start Publishing Content

A vital part of marketing on LinkedIn is creating quality content. This is similar to what is utilized in an affiliate marketing campaign. You can establish blog content on your page. What you create will appear on your company page first, then be shared on news feeds of your followers.

Create engaging and intriguing content if you want people to follow your LinkedIn page. Over time, people become fascinated by your work and start paying attention. Your useful blog posts can be shared, thus leading to more exposure and possibly more visits and sales for your website or retail store.

The blog section is found in the center of your LinkedIn page. The interface is self-explanatory like any other online word processing tool. Write your posts in a separate word processing program, then copy and paste to your LinkedIn profile. Such posts can be very detailed and extensive; you don't want to lose your content while writing it online.

When publishing content:

- Insert related keywords. Keep them relevant and sensible.

- Include content related to what your business is about. Write something inviting and useful while maintaining the interest of the reader.

- Try not to promote your work directly. Just explain to people that you have experience and that you understand what you write about.

- Add updates related to your company. These may include details on new offers, special events and so forth. Do not be overly promotional though. Just state the facts in a simple manner.

- Focus largely on your history when talking about yourself. Instead of what you are doing now, let people know what you have done in the past and how it has led you to where you are today. This is good for letting people know the human side of your work.

Over time, people will start to click on your profile to learn more about your work. Those individuals are familiar with your page and even visit your website or retail location. Others could reach out to you and send private messages about sales, partnerships and other notes. The connections you can develop through your LinkedIn blog will bring more exposure and financial benefits.

Incorporate Media into Your Work

Another way to promote your business is to add media to your regular posts. Rich media creates a dynamic approach that people are bound to love. LinkedIn's official website claims that people are five times more likely to read posts with rich media content.

You can use many things in your LinkedIn blog:

1. While writing a post, click on the box with the plus sign on it. This should be on the top-left part of the writing space.

2. Click on the media you want to include.

You can add the following:

- A still image

- A YouTube video

- A slideshow from SlideShare or another program

- A link to another website; you can enter the text that goes into the link

- A snippet; a special formatting setup for quotes you wish to use from another source provided you correctly attribute the quote.

3. Add a special header to the post. Click the top part of the article or post and select the picture file you want to upload. Keep the header relevant to what your post will be about.

Adding these rich media features makes your video more inviting. The header encourages people to explore your work.

Using LinkedIn is exciting as it brings you to the interest of professionals. Use all the points in this chapter to make your profile and business stand out. Be persistent and meticulous when producing something outstanding. Your efforts are rewarded as visitors begin to value what you share. People will also notice that you have experience and a strong interest in what you are doing, thus making your work even more precious.

Chapter 35 – Advertising on LinkedIn

While using free possibilities to promote yourself on LinkedIn, consider more than just your individual profile. Look at some of the advertisements you could add to your LinkedIn page. These messages help you promote the more popular things you have posted on LinkedIn. With the right ads, you will make your LinkedIn profile and company page noticeable.

There are two types of ads for your social media marketing while on LinkedIn. Let's look at how these work.

Sponsored Updates

The first of the ads you can use on LinkedIn is a sponsored update. This is used for content you want to share with the rest of the world. You could use a sponsored update on any blog post that has received a good amount of feedback or plenty of views. By taking a trendy post into the big time, you are letting people know more about your work.

A sponsored update is a form of native advertising. Your post will go into the feeds of LinkedIn users that you want to contact. It features a header image for your work based on what your choice plus the name of the post. It should also feature a brief description or promotional heading to encourage people to learn what your post is about.

How to prepare your own sponsored update:

1. Go to the LinkedIn Campaign Manager.

2. Link your business account to the manager. To do this, Click on the Add Account button and enter the details of your company page.

3. Enter a name for the account you will promote.

4. List the currency you will use to pay for your update. You can add specific information on how to pay later.

5. Click on the Create Campaign button next to the business account you will use to create your sponsored update.

6. Select the Sponsored Update option.

The other choice is the Text Ads option. That is the second paid advertising choice you can use; details on this are covered later.

7. Enter a name for the sponsored update campaign you will utilize.

8. You have the option to either create a new update or use an existing one from your blog page.

Be advised that you will be unable to edit any existing bits of content.

9. Update the header that will appear on the ad before the user clicks on it.

You can update this based on the picture displayed and the headline for the post among other points.

10. Select the target audience.

The audience is determined by location, age, the size of the company one is associated with, and many other factors. Be as specific as possible.

11. Bid for how much you will spend on each click for your ad.

12. Set a daily budget.

13. Apply a total budget for the life of your ad campaign. You can also list how long you want the campaign to last.

14. Enter your payment information.

15. Launch the campaign. The only charge is for what people actually do with your ads.

Text Ads

The second option for paid marketing on LinkedIn is the text ad. It is a basic ad that includes a reference to your business.

1. Get your account ready for marketing as listed above.

2. Select the Text Ads option in the menu where you choose the campaign.

3. Add the proper name for your new campaign.

4. Determine where people will go when they click your text ad.

You can either get people to visit your website or your LinkedIn page. Specify the URL or LinkedIn site you want someone to access.

5. Add an image to your ad.

6. List a headline and a description. The headline can be 25 characters while a description can be 75.

Make sure you look at the preview before approving anything. That is what people will see when they look at your ad.

7. Create multiple versions of the same ad if you wish.

You can create up to 15 versions.

8. Select the audiences you wish to target.

9. Work with the same payment and budgeting structure as for sponsored updates.

This process lends support for producing an outstanding ad that will be displayed on various pages. A simple routine that is easy to follow.

Using Analytics

Like many other social media sites, LinkedIn has an analytics page that reviews how a marketing campaign is running. The page will include details on how many people are viewing your ads and when they look at them.

Be certain you review the analytics section of your Campaign Manager regularly. The section includes details relating to your project. These include points for:

- How many impressions your ads get.

- The number of clicks each ad has.

- When people click on those ads.

- Details on specific people; this refers to demographics.

- How long people read your sponsored posts.

Use this to identify how each campaign is working. This also helps with reviewing each variation of your posts. It is useful to see how all of those variants of what you add are working. This gives you a clear idea of how well your project is going.

Create Multiple Variations

One thing LinkedIn lets people do with these two options for a paid ad is to create multiple variations of each. You can add several variances based on header images, headlines, text previews and more. The analytics program lets you see how well each edition is operating. Eliminate underperforming versions of an ad and just focus your current campaign on the versions that are working right.

By using these points, it is easier to make LinkedIn a valuable option for your social media marketing. The advertising options on LinkedIn are uncomplicated and do not take much effort to organize.

Chapter 36 – Google Plus

Google is already a useful place that people utilize many times a day. The search engine dominates the industry. However, Google is more than just a great place to find information. It is also a place to market your business. Use Google Plus to help you highlight everything your business has to offer. Google Plus is a social media arm of the popular search engine that can help your business become more visible.

Google Plus has more than 150 million active users. It was created in 2011 as a replacement for Google Buzz, another social media site. The site helps highlight your work and get in touch with others. se it to share information about your business or to start conversations with others.

Become More Visible on Google

Google Plus helps to make your site easier to find on Google searches. Although you can still use Google Plus to get in touch with people, the social media site is best for getting your business and its main website visible on Google. Businesses on Google Plus are more likely to appear at the top of Google searches than others.

This is thanks to Google's algorithm favoring entities that use its services. Google favors videos on YouTube, and businesses with Google Pages are appreciated. People who use more of Google's services will have an easier time making their content visible and easy to use.

Get Local Results

Like with any other search engine, Google heavily focuses on localized traffic. That is, it helps you get in touch with people who are in your local area. Google Plus is ideal for when you are looking for people where you are.

Google has an algorithm that lists local information first when people search for things. For instance, a person in Cincinnati who searches for sporting goods stores or other keywords relating to sporting materials will get results for Cincinnati-area stores and businesses before anything else. This lets the user know there are businesses and retailers in one's local area waiting to do negotiate with them.

Make your business more visible on the search engine when you get on Google Plus. The site reviews your location and makes you more visible to others around that area. Fill out all the proper location data for your business on your profile to get the most out of this. You will learn about getting your address listed later.

Stay in Touch

One part of Google Plus that is popular is the use of circles. Circles are large gatherings of people with whom you might be interested in doing business. You can get your followers to join a circle. This lets you share specific content with particular users. You can use circles to let people know about anything in your business that is unique or special.

Circles are different because you can enlist your members. Add any of your followers into your circles. You could create other circles for different bits of content you wish to send as well. You have the option to use these circles in any way you see fit.

Google Plus is a very attractive social media site worth looking into. It is trouble-free to set up an account with Google Plus and to make it work for you. There are many different aspects of Google Plus that deserve to be explored too. This section of the book will explain how to work with not only a Google Plus page but also with getting other Google-related functions working for you.

Chapter 37 – How to Get Google Plus to Work for You

Google Plus is an undemanding social media site. You can get Google Plus to work quickly and effectively. It only takes a few moments to sign up for Google Plus

Signing Up

As previously mentioned in the YouTube section of this book , the advantages of signing up for Google Plus. You need to get an account with Google Plus to take advantage of everything it offers, including support for YouTube. You can create a new Google Plus profile if you already have a Google account. Then you need to get a brand account that links to your primary one.

To sign up with Google Plus:

1. Click on the Sign In link at plus.google.com.

2. Go to the Create an Account Now link if you do not have a Google account. It is very easy to prepare a user name with Google.

   a. Click on the Sign In button if you just signed up for a Google account. Enter the new user name and password you just created.

3. Enter your real name.

Google Plus asks for your real name to help facilitate better communications between members. If you do not use your actual name, your account could potentially get blocked.

4. List your gender. This is for demographic purposes.

5. Upload a profile photo. You might have to resize the photo. Google Plus lets you select the spot on the photo that you want to use as your profile photo.

6. Click on whether you want Google to use your data for personalized data and content based on what you do.

7. Click the Upgrade button. This allows your Google account to become useful as a Google Plus account.

Getting a Brand Profile

Now that you have created your own Google Plus profile, you need to set up another profile. This one is specifically for your brand. A brand profile helps you make your business stand out. This profile is similar to your personal one, but used for your business instead. This is how you will present your business to others on Google Plus. Your brand account can link up to YouTube as well.

1. Sign in to Google Plus with your current personal account.

2. Go to the left-hand menu and select the Google Plus For Your Brand option.

3. Click on the Create Google Plus page option.

4. Enter a name for your page and brand account. Keep the name as close to your business name as possible.

5. Click the Enable button after reading the terms of use.

Now you have a new brand account ready to use on Google Plus. This account can be used on YouTube when you want to post new videos on the site.

Basic Posting

Posts are important for Google Plus as that is how you will interact with others. A post is a message to communicate. You can use each post to promote anything related to your business, but it is best to write about anything relevant to your business at the start. A keyword-rich post with unique content and valuable information is always worthwhile. This will help people not only to find your content but also more likely to follow your work. You can post various things onto your account or collections.

The process for posting a basic message:

1. Click the pencil-shaped icon on the bottom right of the screen or app.

2. Select where you want the post to go by clicking next to your name.

You can get the post to be visible on your basic page or within an individual collection.

3. Use the body section to enter whatever you want to post.

4. Click the camera icon to upload a photo.

5. Choose the link option to add a URL.

Adding a URL generates a box that displays the logo of the website you are sending people to or a preview of what is on that site. A title and header will also be included. These will list details on what a site is about. Click on the arrow button to change how the box will look; it could be as large or small as you wish.

What Are Those Two Buttons At the Bottom?

There are two buttons at the bottom of each post on your page. A +1 button is included to allow people to show their approval of your work. Your post will get a mark when someone clicks on the +1 button. You can tell your post is popular when you have a high score. You can only get this high score when you have compelling content that is easy to find.

Remember, people are more likely to read and trust Google Plus posts that have more likes. It is up to you to create content that stands out and deserves high numbers.

The other button allows people to forward your posts to Google Plus members they think might enjoy the content. Those members can add their own remarks to a post too. People can share your work to make your content visible to a larger audience. This lets you get the word out about your work without spending money.

Of course, people can always leave comments on your posts. Look at them and try to reply if you can. This shows that you are listening and that you care about what they say.

Adding a Poll

Like with Twitter, you can create a poll on Google Plus. This is perfect when you want to gauge other peoples' opinions. The process for creating a poll on Google Plus is a little different. You have to use a photo directly above the question. This creates a dynamic appearance for the post.

To add a poll to Google Plus:

1. Start up a post.

2. Click on the poll option.

3. Upload a photo to the top part of the poll.

Check on the photo you are adding. It should relate to the poll, but do not create something that would steer people toward one choice. Try to use a photo that evenly displays all the possible choices a person might have.

4. Enter the individual choices you will provide.

5. Click the Add Choice option to add another choice.

Keep doing this for as many choices as you want to create, but try not to have many choices at one time. This is to keep a poll from being too complicated or hard to read.

6. Click the Save button at the bottom.

7. Enter the question you want to ask.

8. Click the Post button at the bottom. Your poll will go live at this point.

This is best for when you want to ask people something about your business or maybe a question relating to what you offer. You can use the responses to your poll to see what people think about something.

Adding a Location

You can also add a location on your Google Plus posts. This is used when you want to target people in a certain area or to specify where your business is located.

1. Turn Google Plus location sharing on. You might have to adjust your mobile device or web browser to allow Google Plus to gain access to your location.

2. Enter details. Be specific.

3. Click on the proper location based on what Google identifies.

Get your business location added to Google to get your specific location listed properly. This is where the next process comes into play.

Enter Your Address

A good idea for making your Google Plus page more visible is to add the address where your business is based. Including this and other bits of contact information is critical to your success. This content can appear on your brand page.

The content is especially important for mobile viewers. People can see your posts and click on the address or information to get additional details. Someone can tap on the address to get directions to your location. That person could also tap on your phone number to call you or tap on an email address to send a message. All of this can be done from the user's mobile phone.

Another Google service to makes this part of Google Plus work for you. This service is Google Places; it is a feature that lets you get your business listed on Google Maps. Add all the details of your contact information through this service:

1. Make sure you log into your Google Plus account.

2. Go to google.com/business to access Google Places.

3. Enter your phone number. Google might be able to find details on your business with that number.

4. Enter the basic information data including points about your location and contact numbers.

5. Mention if you serve customers at your business location.

a. You can choose to hide your mailing address if you do not serve people at the location you specify.

6. Enter the number of miles you are willing to travel to reach customers. This will influence how much of a reach your business has on a search.

7. Add other bits of data to your account as you see fit.

You can add points relating to your hours of operation, payment methods you accept and so forth.

8. Click on the Submit button to get your data verified and secured.

Remember to do this only once. Do not do it multiple times if you have several locations. You can enter multiple service areas while filling out your account if you have enough spots to work with.

It might take some time for Google to verify your data. There have been some cases where Google has sent verification notices to physical addresses. Such instances are rare, but you might have to wait two or three weeks to get your content verified. The wait will be worth it as your Google Plus content will be easier for people to spot when your location information is listed properly.

Creating Content

Google Plus lets you generate content to market your business. This works as you will create collections that might feature numerous posts or other bits of information related to your business.

You have the option to create individual posts that are not part of collections. However, it is always wise to add collections to help you make your content more distinct. Collections let you store posts that are related to one another.

Creating a collection is effortless:

1. Go to your Profile page.

2. Click on the Create a Collection on the screen.

3. Enter a name for the collection.

4. Determine to whom you want to make the collection visible.

You can allow the collection to be visible to everyone on Google Plus or just to people in your circles. You can customize the reach of your collection too.

5. Enter a tagline. This should be relevant to the content in the collection.

6. After clicking to create the collection, you can add a custom photo to the top. This header shows people what the collection is about before clicking on it.

This header photo needs to be descriptive and related to the collection. More importantly, it should be inviting. Look for an exciting image that might be attractive to your reader.

7. Click whether you want your circles to follow your new collection automatically.

8. Click the Save button.

Remember that creating enough quality content and getting more followers on your Google Plus page helps you make the most out of this social media avenue. In fact, the followers you get can become a part of a circle, a point you will read about in the next chapter.

Chapter 38 – Setting Up Circles

One important aspect of Google Plus for marketing involves how you can use it to create strong communities. Circles are the larger communities that you can start up on Google Plus. These are communities that people can get benefit from, but will not know that they are actually in the said group.

A circle is a grouping to share various posts. Add other people into a circle and have those members read what you have posted online. The best part is that you have full control over who is invited.

The people in your circle have access to all the content you are posting. Add any kind of post or collection you want to your circle. You could send notifications about anything you have added to your basic site. You can also get content sent only to your circle. This is ideal if you want to create more personal or professional relationships with others.

Use the circle to follow content that offers something of interest. This includes new posts from other members. This is great if you have many people in your circle that you admire.

Even more importantly, a circle will help you contact individuals with whom you want to set up business partnerships. Your circle allows you to interact with people who have similar interests and to share proposals and plans with you. This could be critical for getting a large long-term project running.

The best part is that you can use the circle to get in touch with people through not only Google Plus but also via emails. You will learn more about the email aspect of Google Plus in the next chapter.

Get People to Follow Your Google Plus Page

A Google Plus circle is ideal for sharing content. To make a circle work, get people to follow your Google Plus account. To do that, you have to produce content that people want to follow.

To attract followers:

- Create unique posts and collections that will interest people. Show that your work is unique and people will want to follow what you do as a result.

- Follow other peoples' Google Plus pages if possible. Follow ones that related to yours. This shows that you like what someone else is offering.

- Post comments on other peoples' pages.

- Be consistent with your updates.

- Create content that will be useful for a time. It is easier for people to follow your work if you have more evergreen content.

Many of these points are universal tips for use on any social media site. However, they are suggestions that everyone should be using anyway.

Creating a Circle

You can create a circle after you have amassed enough followers.

To create your circle:

1. Open your Google Plus page.

2. Go to the People section on your menu.

3. Click on the Following section to see who is following your page.

4. Choose the New Circle option.

5. Enter a name for your circle.

The people who follow your page are automatically placed in your circle.

6. Add people to your circle by tapping their profiles and selecting to add them. You can use the same option to remove people.

Sharing Content in Your Circle

You can share posts with particular circles you have created. This might be useful if you have multiple circles, but you only want your content to show up in one circle at a time.

1. Go to the People section of your account.

2. Click on the Following option.

3. Click on the Circle Settings section.

4. Tap on the boxes that specify the circles where you want to share your content.

This keeps you from using the default Your Circles option when prompted to share new posts or collections with other people. The Your Circles option automatically assumes that you have your content shared to every circle you created. By adjusting the setting, you will keep your content from going out to every circle. This is vital if you only want to target a certain grouping and not each of your circles.

A Note About Privacy

An interesting part of Google Plus circles is that each circle is fully private. A person who is in a circle will not get information on whoever else is in that circle. People in the circle do not even know the name of the group or the purpose of that group. Those people will still get the content you offer. The point is that you are using your circle to find out who is following your page, thus helping you create content people want to read and share with others.

What About Extended Circles?

Extended circles may be available as well. When you choose to share things with people in your circle, you might have the option to get that content out to an extended circle. This community features people who are in circles within your individual circle. For instance, your work is posted not only to ones in your circles but also the people who are in circles created by those same followers.

The grouping of people in your extended circles varies based on who your followers include in their own circles. You will not have access to details on who they are. Be aware of this when getting your circles ready and sending content out to people who aren't necessarily in your circles.

Whenever possible always use circles for Google Plus. Circles are vital to your success and allow people to see what you offer and why it is valuable. Get enough followers so you can create your own circles.

Chapter 39 – Sending Emails Through Gmail

Email marketing is just as important to your business' success as social media marketing. You can use emails to reach people and let them know about anything you have to offer. Today you can use Google Plus alongside Gmail to get emails sent out to people who follow you. This is a great mix between email and social media marketing that improves your chances of reaching people and sending detailed information.

About Gmail

The main aspect of email marketing through Google Plus is Gmail. Google uses this popular program for standard email communications. Perhaps you already have a Gmail account. More than a billion people have Gmail accounts, so the odds are good you have used Gmail yourself or have run into a Gmail address in the past.

Gmail is a free program that lets you send and receive emails. You can use Gmail to add files from a Google Drive cloud storage account to your emails or to forward information on YouTube videos. You can even use Google Hangouts right through your Gmail desktop. You also have the option to use the Gmail mobile app to review and send messages. The simplicity of Gmail makes it a favorite among people looking to send emails as quickly as possible.

So, how does this all relate to Google Plus? You can use your account to send special messages to persons within your Google Plus circles.

Why Get Gmail Linked to Google Plus?

There are several good reasons to get Gmail to work with your Google Plus account:

- Any recent posts you have made on your Google Plus page will appear on the Gmail widget. These can be included in any Gmail message you send others, thus allowing your posts to be read by more people.

- Gmail recipients who are already on Google Plus can see follow buttons on your emails. This will encourage your recipients to follow your page.

- Your logo will become more visible on any email you send.

- Most importantly, your emails will help people learn more about what you do provided you write emails that are informative and detailed. People are more likely to check their Gmail accounts than their Google Plus accounts. Linking your work to Gmail helps you get the word out to people even when they aren't signed in.

How to Get Your Page Linked to Gmail

Get your Google Plus page to connect to Gmail with a few quick steps:

1. Go to business.google.com.

Apply for an account with Google Business if you do not have one. It is free and easy to do. You have to list contact information and website details as well as other information.

2. Go to the My Business menu and select your Google Plus page.

3. Click the About tab.

4. Go to the Link My Website option.

5. Wait for the webmaster to verify your request.

6. You will get an email notifying that you have been accepted.

At this point, you should get your Gmail account linked to Google Plus. Now you can use Gmail to get in touch with everyone in your circle.

Specify when writing a message that you want it sent to people within your circle. This will automatically identify the email addresses within that circle, and the message will be sent. This offers a simple approach to marketing to get specific emails out to the individuals you want to target.

What if You Have Many Gmail Accounts?

Maybe your business has a Gmail account for every person in your workplace. You can get all of them to link to Google Plus. Specifically, use this to create a private circle that links all of these Gmail profiles. This allows you to correspond with others in the business through Google Plus.

This process requires you to work with Yahoo's mail system. This is a bit of a trick, but it takes advantage of an intriguing feature of Google Plus. You can use the social media site to find friends from Yahoo. This works by clicking on a Yahoo Mail account and getting the contacts from these added into your Google Plus feed.

1. Log into a Gmail account not associated with Google Plus.

2. Go to the Contacts section. Make sure you have all your company's Gmail accounts in that section.

3. Export your contacts into a CSV file.

4. Use a Yahoo Mail account. You might have to create a dummy account if you don't have one.

5. Go to the Contacts section of Yahoo Mail.

6. Click to import your contacts. Use the CSV file you just prepared.

7. Start up your Google Plus profile.

8. Click on the Find Friends section and select Yahoo.

9. You can now get the contacts from that Yahoo Mail account imported over.

With this, you can get your messages sent out to all the people in your business. You could create a circle that includes everyone who has a Gmail account in particular.

Chapter 40 – Using Google Hangouts For a Video Chat

One valuable part of using Google Plus is a special program that lets you chat with others in real time. This program is Google Hangouts, a communication app that facilitates live chats. Google Hangouts is a live instant messaging and video chat program that connects to your Google Plus page. Use Hangouts to interact in real time and set up special events.

More importantly, you can use a video chat on Google Hangouts to teach people about your work. Whether it is VIPs who want early access to your work or just a need to talk with associates or partners, Google Hangouts makes chatting easy. Best of all, it is not difficult to set up provided you have the equipment ready.

Google Hangouts works with a simple layout. Click on the proper Hangouts app on your mobile device or open it on the Gmail page on your browser. Click the quotation-shaped symbol and look for whom you want to chat with. After that, you can talk with people in real time. This is a useful application that does not require technical skills.

This serves especially well to get in touch with particular individuals. You can even invite people within your Google Plus circles to join your chat.

This chapter is on how to use the video chat feature on Google Hangouts. While it is true that you can send text messages to people on Hangouts, it is even better to chat with them by video. A video chat lets you interact in a persuasive way. You can answer text messages during the chat or even talk with others who have their own webcams or mobile devices.

Two Quick Notes

Only Google account holders have access to Google Hangouts. Before you start a session always mention that to participate a Google account is required. Fortunately, Google is so common that most people have a Gmail account by now. Share your plans ahead of time just to be safe.

There is a limit to how many people can be on your Hangout. Only 100 people can visit your Hangout at a time. Choose carefully when figuring out whom you want to chat with. Try to invite individuals to your Hangout from the start. Think about how important they are to your business; to share the information at that time or can you invite them later?

How to Use Google Hangouts

A Google Hangout is perfect for when you have Google Plus members or other people that you want to talk to in real time. Here are a few situations where a Google Hangout video chat is great to utilize:

- Chat with possible business partners through Hangouts. You can use this to talk about details relating to a huge endeavor you want to set up. This might be more effective than just exchanging one private post after another.

- Make a big announcement about your business through your Hangout. The small audience at your Hangout could be the first to know about what you are doing. Choose to get the news out to the rest of the world a few hours or days later.

- A Hangout is great for interviews. Interview someone who wants to join your business as an employee.

- Members of the staff or other business associates can discuss upcoming events through a Hangout. A monthly meet-up would help, and everyone in the business gets on the same page.

All of these suggestions are great for marketing. Plan future marketing ideas with your employees, or a partnership. Sometimes that personal touch created through your chat will motivate someone to feel confident in what you offer. A video chat will help you get online fast while interacting with anyone you think has significance.

Promote a Hangout

When using Google Hangouts, tell people on Google Plus about starting a Hangout. You could always go to other social media sites and mention the Hangout session too. Make sure people know when your Hangout meeting will be ready and what it will cover.

Get people to sign up to access the Hangout. Specify the particular Google Plus account they should contact on the Hangouts menu. This tells them your plans for the big event.

Starting a Hangout

When the time for your meeting comes along, get your Hangout started on Google Plus. You have one of many options for getting your Hangout ready:

1. You can go to Gmail to start your chat.

Just go to the Hangouts icon on your Gmail page to get your chat ready.

2. You can also use the Hangouts extension on Google Chrome.

Google offers a free Hangouts extension to use on the Chrome web browser. Go to chrome.google.com/webstore to download the extension.

3. The Hangouts app will also work on your mobile device.

Hangouts should be available on most Android devices. You download it from a proper online store through your operating system if you do not have it. Fortunately, it works on both the Android and iOS systems.

Select a Group Conversation

Start your chat by using the group conversation feature.

1. Click on the New Conversation option.

2. Enter the contact details for the people who will chat with you. These include Google Plus profiles.

3. Name your conversation if appropriate.

4. Click the green check.

5. You can also add people to your group later on if desired. Click the person-shaped icon and enter the data on who enters the chat. You can also do the same to anyone in your group that you wish to remove.

Send Links to Join

Send links to other Google Plus pages before your Hangout starts:

1. Click the gear-shaped settings icon on Hangouts.

2. Select the Join By Link box.

3. Click the Copy Link box.

4. Share that link. You can post this on Google Plus pages or other social media sites.

Get the links sent as soon as possible. Also, bring up when the Hangout event takes place. Getting the links ready before the Hangout will validate your approaching event. This is great if you have been promoting your Hangout for a while and want people to visit as soon as possible.

Check Your Camera

Make sure you get the proper camera ready for your Hangout session. You need a camera that is as clear and as professional as possible. Also, ensure that it is a high-definition model that will not shake or struggle to pick up audio. Although a camera built into a laptop or a webcam works, you are better off connecting a larger professional camera to your computer. This is to make your feed a little more detailed.

Starting and Ending the Chat

It is easy to get the chat started at the precise time.

1. Open up the Hangout app or extension.

2. Select the name of the conversation that you want to start up. Make sure you enter the proper names of the people you want to talk to.

3. Click the camera icon. This should let you get the chat started.

At this point, you have access to the people with whom you want to chat. Others on the site should join the same chat in a while.

4. Click on the phone icon to end the chat.

Remember that the same rules for chatting with people on YouTube or Facebook apply to Hangouts on Google Plus. Always interact with people and politely respond to any comments. Address people by name and be encouraging or insightful. Let everyone at the event know that you appreciate them watching.

Your Google Hangout will help you get in touch with many people. This is great for talking with someone in your circle or anyone interested in certain business functions you want to set up. Try this option when self-marketing on Google Plus. It is like having a full conversation with people but in a virtual environment.

Chapter 41 – Using AdWords and +Post Ads on Google Plus

This chapter focuses on two particular options for paid marketing on Google Plus. They are ideal if you are adding regular marketing work to your Google Plus page, but you may still need some help. The two choices are to use Google AdWords on your page or to create +Post ads. Both can help you create an outstanding ad set that gets people to click designated links to reach your page.

Working with AdWords

AdWords is a vital part of Google that every person on the site should review. AdWords is a system used by Google to help businesses promote their goods and services. Chapter 19 discussed how to use AdWords. To refresh your memory, this is where a business provides a limit to the money expended connecting their links to certain keywords. A business then gets the links associated with the keywords. That business will make a monetary payment every time someone clicks an advertisement.

AdWords is effective because it is simple to use. Businesses of all sorts use AdWords to make them visible. The fact that you can get an account set up quickly while setting a limit for what you would spend makes AdWords all the more valuable and ideal to use.

You can get AdWords to link to your Google Plus page. By doing this, you will make the AdWords system easier to utilize. Use AdWords to market your website or your Google Plus page. Or use it to highlight another social media site you are using. The key is to get it linked to keywords that relate to your business efforts and content.

Google AdWords allows you to control the ads you put on your Google Plus page. You have full advantage over the ads by having your messages appear first. These will show up on your page instead of anything else that some other entity might try to post. In other words, you have full control over your promotions.

How to Get a Link Ready

To have AdWords link to your Google Plus page:

1. Go to the Google AdWords site. Log into your account.

2. Create an AdWords campaign to use on your Google Plus page.

The campaign needs to be programmed with proper keywords in mind. You have the option to specify particular Google Plus posts that you want to highlight over all others on your page too.

3. Click on the Ad Extensions tab.

4. Go to the View: Social Extensions option. This should be on the left side of the screen.

5. Click the New Extension option.

6. Click on the AdWords campaign that you want to use.

7. Enter the URL of your Google Plus page.

8. The AdWords campaign should link to the Google Plus page you created.

What Should be Promoted Most?

Check your Google Plus page when looking for posts you could promote through AdWords. You have the option to select a specific post on your page that would link to your AdWords page. Anything that performs well and gets lots of interaction is clearly best. Check your entire catalog of posts to see what works.

Using a +Post Ad

The second option for paid advertising is to use a +Post ad. This lets you promote Google Plus posts on the search engine in the same way that you would with a traditional ad. This is effective if you have a particular message you wish to express.

To make this work, you need to produce new and rich media content. You can prepare your content in one of three forms:

1. Set up a hover-to-play ad. This is where a video will play when a person hovers their mouse cursor over the video box.

2. A one video lightbox could pop up when a person goes to a certain Google Plus page. This creates a video display in the center of the screen. The user can choose to load it and watch the video or not.

3. Your Google Plus content can also be posted with a basic layout similar to how an AdWords text ad is incorporated into a Google search. This option is best if you want to reach people who do visit Google Plus sites. It provides you with the best possible reach, but it does not contain the rich media that the other two options feature.

All options will be displayed with a standard layout that lets people click the +1 button to like something or the opportunity to leave a comment.

Each of these options is worthwhile, but check the content you wish to work with. You can use the third choice if you have a Google Plus post that is popular and you feel it needs to be posted on more sites. If you wish, you can also highlight a brief video advertisement related to your business. Regardless, use the +Post feature to create something outstanding.

How Many Followers?

You need at least a thousand followers on your Google Plus page to use the +Post advertising option. Google Plus only allows experienced users access to its more advanced advertising components.

Steps for Use

To get a +Post ad ready:

1. Go to the Google Plus Create an Ad page. Visit plus.google.com/+googleads to get started.

2. Select the campaign type you want to utilize.

The best option for Google Plus is to engage with the audience. You can also promote a mobile app or remarket something with your ad, but the best option is to choose the engagement choice.

3. Select the ad format.

4. Enter a name for your ad.

5. Upload the content or select the post you want to use.

6. Click to display comments on your post. This is best if you have many positive comments on that post.

7. Preview your advertisement on the right-hand side of the screen. This should list what your ad will look like based on how big or small you want the page to be.

8. Set up your budget for the ad campaign. You should have details on how much each exposure will be worth.

You may be billed based on the number of clicks to your link or how long someone watches a video. In the case of a video, you will be billed when someone hovers over the ad for three seconds (naturally, you need to grab the viewer's attention at the very beginning to make it worthwhile).

Reviewing Analytics

Do not forget to look at the analytics for this marketing ploy. Your +Post analytics will display the follow statistics:

- The number of times your post was viewed or received interaction.

- The +1 remarks left on your post as a result of your campaign.

- How many times people shared your ad.

- Comments that were added to your post.

- Any extra social actions that were utilized.

Using paid advertising on Google Plus is uncomplicated. Whether it is for AdWords or the +Post system, you are bound to get more people look at your site when the proper campaign is set up.

Chapter 42 – Reddit

Reddit is a fascinating and fun place to be online. Reddit is a site where people can talk about all kinds of subjects through a number of subsections. The diversity of what people can discuss on Reddit is practically endless.

Reddit is a social aggregator that was created in 2005. The site is a place where people can post news stories and other things that interest them. The site has grown to include around 500 million visitors each month with about 230 million unique users from all around the world. The site is immensely popular, and nearly 80 billion page views take place on the site every year.

How Reddit Works

To understand how to use Reddit for your marketing, you should find out how Reddit works. Here are a few steps someone would use to get something onto Reddit:

1. Find a news story or other topic of interest. In some cases, you might come up with a unique post.

A person could submit an existing story, link from somewhere online, or create a post.

2. That user, or redditor, would submit the post to a particular subreddit.

A subreddit is a part of Reddit where people can talk about a very specific thing. Subreddits are amazingly diverse and cover everything from news to entertainment to sports and various hobbies or themes.

3. A title must be written by the redditor.

The title needs to be catchy and interesting. It must draw people into the post.

4. A thumbnail may be included. This would preview a picture that someone can view by clicking on the title.

5. After the content is submitted, people can click on the link. They will be taken to a new page on Reddit either where the content is located or another website.

You can use this to post a link to your website. You could also create a story or other long-form post.

6. People can click on the comments box to leave remarks about what they are seeing.

As with other social media sites, you have the option to respond to comments as you see fit.

7. Users can also click the Share button to send the content to another social media site or to create an embedded link leading to the post.

8. People can also click the up or down arrows on the left-hand side of the post. This is to indicate if someone likes or dislikes the post.

The posts with the most likes will be easier to spot on a subreddit. This is a sign that the Reddit community at large is appreciative of something.

The process for using Reddit is simple and gives you a golden opportunity to market yourself. You can get anything posted on Reddit so long as it involves your business. Whether it leads directly to your website or it has some other bit of content, the things you can add to Reddit are basically infinite.

Who Uses Reddit?

It is not difficult to find an audience on Reddit. It is estimated by Statista that there are nearly 1.2 million subreddits on the site. Each subreddit is devoted to a particular topic of interest. Perhaps you can find one on the site that relates to your interest and business.

In terms of demographics, there are many interesting things to explore. The demographic statistics are based on a 2016 Pew Research Center study:

- Around two-thirds of Reddit users are male.

- Two-thirds of users are in the 18-29 age range.

- About 40% of people on the site have a college degree. Another 40% have some college experience.

- The earning power of people on Reddit is surprisingly diverse. The site is spread out from people who earn more than $75,000 a year to those who earn $25,000 or less.

Overall, Reddit is great to find younger people to whom you want to market your business. Every subreddit is different. Some places might cater to older people, although those might be a challenge to locate. Search Reddit to see which subreddits might be of value to you.

Chapter 43 – Finding the Right Spot on Reddit

Before you start promoting yourself on Reddit, look for a great place to promote your business. With more than a million subreddits, it can be challenging to find the right one.

That is the beauty of Reddit. With this social media site, you can communicate with people about anything. The odds are there is a subreddit out there that offers something in which you have a strong interest.

How to Search for a Subreddit

The best way to discover a good place to post on Reddit is to search for a particular subreddit. You can use Reddit's search engine to find a section that is devoted to the specific things you want to highlight. Here's how to use the search feature to find something of value:

1. Go to the More section at the top part of the Reddit website.

2. Enter what you want to experience.

3. Look at the listing to see what is included.

Each listing should include the name of the subreddit, a description, and the number of subscribers.

4. You can also click or tap the Subscribe button to subscribe to a subreddit you might want to use.

Look at the many subreddits available for your use. You might be surprised at the various options you have for getting online. The options are vast. Just look through the list to see what is available and consider how you can use it to your advantage.

How Specific Should the Audience Be

An interesting thing about subreddits is that they can are about all sorts of things. After a while, you will go from a generic audience to a specific one. This audience would be smaller, but it would be united by the topic.

Go to the Television section of Reddit, for instance. That page has about 14 million people viewing it right now. This is a massive audience of people talking about television in general. When you click on specific subreddits devoted to very specific shows or television genres, that audience becomes smaller. The subreddit for the Walking Dead has only 440,000 people on it while the subreddit for Rick and Morty has about 700,000 people. Something even less popular would have even fewer people on it; for instance, the subreddit for Crazy Ex-Girlfriend has less than 10,000 people on it.

Something to notice The general disparity between subreddits over how many followers they have. When looking for National Hockey League teams, you will observe that the subreddits for the Chicago Blackhawks and Montreal Canadiens have more followers than the ones for the Carolina Hurricanes and Vegas Golden Knights. This example suggests a popularity contest always continues on Reddit and that certain concepts are much more intriguing to Reddit users than others are. When you get into something specific, the popularity or interest will vary. Some lists have much smaller audiences than others.

Be specific about the people you want to reach. For instance, you might be running a business dedicated to selling and restoring old video game consoles. You might want to target people on subreddits that relate to classic video games instead of ones that talk about the latest games. Subreddits that involve specific video game consoles from the past could be valuable to highlight your business.

Always choose a subreddit focused on what you do and the target audience you want. Never ignore your overall goals when planning your Reddit efforts. Look at how well the subreddits you choose are organized, so you get your work to stand out.

Chapter 44 – Planning Your Reddit Posts

Now that you have found a subreddit or two to use for sharing your work, get your Reddit posts ready. Look at your plans for having the site work for you. Only offer great posts that will draw people to your site or get people to learn more.

Direct Link or Text Post?

There are two types of posts you can produce on Reddit. First, you can create a post links directly to a website. This might be your own website. Second, you can use a longer text post. This leads people to a new page of Reddit where you are displaying more text about your business and maybe a photo or YouTube video.

A link-based post is best if you want to get more people to your site. This is when your business is recognizable, or you have a sensible heading that will draw people to your site. We'll talk about the headings later.

A text post is better if you want to explain yourself a little more or to create some links. You can add links to your site within your extended post. More importantly, your post tells others what makes your work special and why they should trust you.

Create an Attractive but not Promotional Profile

Start your Reddit marketing by creating a profile. Avoid having a profile that looks like something a business would generate. Rather, establish a profile that looks as though a real person is posting things on Reddit, not a business. Reddit will become suspicious if you directly post things as a business entity.

To create an acceptable Reddit profile:

1. Go to the official Reddit website.

2. Click the sign-up box.

3. Enter your email address.

Try to use an email address that is separate from any business-oriented ones. An email address with a Ymail, Gmail, or Yahoo domain will be easier to trust as it does not appear to be made with a business in mind.

4. Click on a series of communities to which you want to subscribe.

Choose to subscribe with a series of subreddits if desired. Reddit will provide you with multiple options to sign up. Subscribe to at least five of them. Look for ones that relate to your business.

5. Select a username and then enter a password.

6. Go to your profile page to add a display name and description of yourself.

Keep this casual without sounding as if you are advertising a product or service.

7. Add an avatar that will be associated with your posts if you like.

This should not be the logo of your business. It could be an avatar of yourself if you wish. People might take your work more seriously if you create an avatar.

How to Submit a Post

Now that you have a profile ready, you can start by submitting posts on Reddit. Don't post anything related to your business just yet. Start by creating insightful and thoughtful posts about whatever interests you. This demonstrates that you are careful with your posts and not rushing things on Reddit.

Link-Based Post

First, let's talk about getting a link-based post online. This can help you bring people to your own site. Avoid promoting your site at the start, as it will be explained later.

1. Go to the subreddit you want to add a post on.

2. Click the link option.

3. Read the rules for the subreddit to which you are posting. Each subreddit has its own standards for what you can and cannot post.

4. Enter the URL of whatever you want to link people to.

5. Add an image or video if desired.

The image or video could be used as a header that appears next to the link. When someone clicks on the comment section, they will see the image or video in detail.

6. Enter a title.

The title should be a descriptor of what people see on the link. Make the title as creative as possible. Give a summary of what's on it or maybe make a brief non-promotional statement about what is on that link.

7. Confirm the subreddit that you are adding the post.

8. You also have the option to receive replies to your post sent to your profile inbox.

Your link post will let people know about something interesting on a different website. This is perfect if you can think of something related to your business. It tells people you care about something that involves your business.

Text Post

You can also create a text post on Reddit. This is a post where you explain something in a more detail. It has a title people will read before clicking, and then something larger after the post is opened. Think of it as a blog post, but instead it is on a subreddit for everyone to see. Here are some steps to apply:

1. Click to add a post to a subreddit.

2. Choose the text post option.

3. Enter the title or heading using the same standards from earlier.

4. Write your content in a word processing tool.

5. Add rich media to your content as you see fit.

6. Click to confirm the subreddit where you will post this content.

7. Send to the subreddit.

Now you just have to wait and see how people respond. Watch for the comments and any upvotes. You might have a frontrunner on your hands if people are willing to upvote and support your work.

Get Enough Karma

You must get enough karma on your account before you begin promoting your work. Karma is a measurement of activity on Reddit. It explains to people how much work someone puts into activities on the site.

Karma is vital for showing you have a strong link. You can gain karma by both posting things on Reddit and interacting with other peoples' posts. It will be easier for you to get karma if you do enough positive things on the site and display a good attitude. Don't forget to choose subreddits that relate to your business as they will be more interesting and valuable for your promotional needs.

What to Avoid

It is easier to get kicked off of Reddit than it is to be trusted by people on the site. Reddit is notorious for having a tough policy; people who abuse the system are banned from the site. The site has a very strict anti-spam policy. It does not desire people to use the site for promotional purposes. It wants people to be inventive and thoughtful without trying to promote their business directly to people.

Here are some of the things you need to avoid doing when on Reddit:

- Do not sound promotional. Refrain from using marketing-type language.

- Never share anyone's private information with others. In other words, don't share your contact number, address, or other details with people on Reddit.

- Don't ask people to give you upvotes. Let those upvotes come to you naturally.

- Watch for the links you produce. Add links going to many places and not just your website.

- Avoid submitting your content onto multiple subreddits. Pick only one subreddit and remain with that one if possible. You can add different posts to other subreddits provided they are radically different and are about different concepts or topics.

Chapter 45 – Hosting an AMA or IAmA Event

You can use Reddit to talk all about your work. This can come from either the AMA or IAmA subreddits. These are two different subreddits with unique focal points, but they are alike in that people can discuss who they are and share interesting information. Hosting an event at one of these two places is always great to consider.

A Quick Note

Try to get more karma on Reddit before you host an event. Although anyone can have an event, the people with the most karma on Reddit are often the most trusted. These users are active and enjoy talking about many things of interest or relevance to them. Be active on Reddit so it becomes easier for your page to stand out.

AMA Events

An AMA event is an Ask Me Anything event. The AMA subreddit hosts all of them. During an AMA session, you will go online and tell people that you are doing something or that you have experience in an activity. You will then have people who want to ask you some questions.

As the questions arise, you will answer them with clear responses. This is great for promotional efforts provided you know how to host an event like this.

AMA events often include interesting things. Just look at the AMA subreddit and note the discussions to ask people about:

- Significant events in their life.

- Certain work experiences people have had.

- Exceptional things people are doing right now.

Use your AMA event to talk about what you have been working on.

To host your AMA event:

1. Go to reddit.com/r/ama to get started.

2. Click on the button to start an AMA.

3. Enter a title.

The title should be attractive and specific. For instance, a person who runs a lawn care business could have a title that says "I have a professional lawn care service and do lots of lawn work. AMA." This title gives the reader an idea of what you will discuss.

4. Add a text description people will read after clicking the title. This is optional but recommended.

The description could include a few details about your skill set; what you specifically do in your work or business. Avoid being overly promotional in this section.

5. Confirm that your AMA will go into the AMA subreddit. You could also get this posted on another subreddit if desired.

6. Wait for the comments to follow. Be sure to respond to them quickly so people know you are there and willing to provide answers.

IAmA Events

You can host an IAmA event after you develop a larger presence on Reddit, and have enough karma to credibly host an IAmA. Think of the IAmA subreddit as a formal side of

Reddit where credible people talk with others about their ideas.

An IAmA event is what it sounds like – you are telling others "I am a…"

It is a extra detailed event. If anything, an IAmA event is a more formal approach to the AMA. This is where you debate the technical points of what you do.

Over the years, IAmA events became very popular on Reddit. They are so big that many celebrities often go to Reddit to talk about their work through the subreddit. They take questions from various people and share tidbits about the things they do. You don't have to be a celebrity to use this subreddit. You just need to have a good presence with plenty of karma and a more detailed layout for your chat.

To get an IAmA session ready:

1. Go to reddit.com/r/iama to get to the subreddit.

2. Click the link to submit an IAmA chat.

3. Enter the name of the chat.

The best template is "IAmA (what you do). AMA." Going back to the original lawn care example, you could say "IAmA lawn care professional with years of experience. Have you ever wondered what you can do to get your lawn to look its best? AMA.

4. Enter a short biography.

The biography should include details on what you do. Do not list your specific business in the bio; just talk about how you work and maybe add a link to your site. When you add that link, just say something like "You can learn more about what I do at (domain name).

5. Submit proof relating to you getting your IAmA session ready.

You will have to get an image uploaded to Imgur to get your proof ready. Imgur is a free site that lets you host images to share on various websites including social media pages. Take a picture of yourself for your testimony. Hold up a sign with a message promoting your IAmA event and the day that it is scheduled to be held.

6. Submit the IAmA to Reddit.

It might take some time for Reddit to accept your event because they get many requests. You should receive a response stating that your IAmA is accepted. You may wait an hour or two for the event to be ready. Try to get the occasion submitted to Reddit a few hours before the time you are on Reddit to ensure you will actually be live at the time you have chosen.

After you get the event started, you can chat with others on Reddit. Spend a bit of time talking to people and answering questions. This is a fun way to interact and get the word out about what you are doing. The fact that it is free makes it especially intriguing.

Should You Mention Your Specific Business?

You can always talk to people about what you do with your business during one of these events on Reddit. Whatever you do, never promote it directly. Casually mention that your work is listed on a certain website, but that should be all. The content within your event will lead people to click the link you added. In short, keep your AMA or IAmA event focused and straightforward without delving into promotional details.

Promote Your Event

Your AMA or IAmA event cannot be scheduled to materialize at a certain time. Only big-name celebrities and personalities who get in touch with Reddit to promote events can do this. Rather, you have to get your post added to either subreddit at a certain time. You have the option to add your event at any moment you wish. You just cannot schedule beforehand when the content is going to show up.

The best way to promote your event is to let people know that you will be holding such a chat. Post messages on your official website and other social media accounts you have , announcing that you will be holding a Reddit event. Let people know a few days in advance so they have time to visit and see what you have to say. This also helps them coming up with questions to ask you.

Moreover, whatever you do, never endorse your event directly on Reddit. This would be a blatant example of self-promotion that Reddit frowns upon. Stick with other social media sites you have.

How Long Should the Event Last?

When you post on the IAmA or AMA subreddits, your event will last for as long as it has to. It will appear on the site forever until you personally choose to delete. The event doesn't have to last forever. After you commence the AMA or IAmA event you can talk with people for a few hours. You could even respond to some comments a day or two later if things slowed down.

Ultimately, update the main post when you are finished. Let people know that the event is closed and you will not answer anything else. You can thank people for their time and even add a link to your site provided it has no promotional overtones.

Closing Your Event

Don't forget to close your chat. Although your chat will not vanish, there is always a chance that it remains open if you d not adjust the settings. That means people could still ask you questions months or even years later unless you close the chat. Granted, it would not be likely to get questions after all that time, but there is always the potential for it to happen.

To close your AMA or IAmA event:

1. Edit your description in the event stating that it is closed. This should preemptively keep people from trying to post anything.

2. Click the button near the Delete and NSFW buttons on your post.

3. Click the Flair section.

4. Choose the Closed option.

5. Now it displays that your event is closed. This should block people from being able to chat. You can always reopen the event in the future by removing the Closed option from your posting.

Additional Tips

Here are a few extra tips when hosting one of these Reddit events:

- Be transparent, but know your limits. Don't reveal industry secrets or anything that might be too surprising.

- Have a sense of personality in your work. Show your unique attitude to let people know your interest in your vocation.

- Do not be afraid to discuss some of the negative concerns over what you do, but do not dwell on them. Anything that is too negative or persistent could be troubling to some.

- Watch for anyone who might be difficult or hard to manage in your discussion. You can click any name to block that person from your chat if you have to.

The IAmA and AMA subreddits are perfect for your Reddit marketing. These let you talk with people about everything you do. It is all about providing a closer look at what you are doing and what makes your work outstanding for someone to read and use.

Chapter 46 – Getting a Paid Ad on Reddit

While you should not be directly promoting your business in the posts you add on Reddit, there is one option for directly marketing your business. This involves getting a paid advertisement on Reddit. A paid ad will prominently appear on a Reddit feed. This works as it produces a link to your website. The ad includes a few points for simple use:

- The ad features a title that looks like an ordinary headline.

- A picture that relates to the title or your site may be included.

- Details of the URL is listed.

- The name of whoever is promoting the ad could be mentioned as well.

This is an attractive option for advertising. However, this part of social media marketing should be used carefully. Know where the campaign will work and how you are going to produce quality ads in the campaign. Your efforts to create a good ad on Reddit will make a difference if you make it outstanding and attractive.

How to Get Your Ad Ready

It is easy to plan a Reddit ad:

1. Sign in to your Reddit account.

2. Go to ads.reddit.com to get started on producing your advertisements.

3. Create a name for your campaign.

4. Prepare the advertisement.

Have a good title for the ad. It could be something relating to your company. The title or headline can only be up to 100 characters in length.

5. Get an image to display.

You also need an image for the ad. You need both; a thumbnail image of 140x140 and a mobile card view image of 1200x628. This is to make your work visible on a mobile device.

6. Select your target audience.

The options you have for targeting your audience on Reddit include:

- Specific subreddits.

- Geographic locations where people are based.

- Interests that individual users have; these relate to the subreddits to which those people are subscribed.

- Any specific platforms you want your ads to appear on; you can get your ad on a desktop display or just on a mobile device.

- The specific mobile operating system; this works if you are trying to promote an app that only works on one system.

7. Determine the time of day when you want your ads to appear. Adjust the settings so the ad will show up based on the time and day of the week.

A full chart is listed to help you sort out the timing.

8. Set a budget for your ad.

You can place a bid for how much you want to spend for every 1,000 impressions your ad produces. You could also set up a daily budget for how much you are willing to spend per day. Another option is to set the campaign beginning and ending dates if you want to keep your work controlled. Examine how much the campaign will be worth to you and how much you are willing to spend.

Avoid Being Too Direct

A good key for your paid ad is to keep your message from being too direct. You can create a title that involves your business without stating point-blank that you have something to sell. You might use keywords involving your business while explaining to visit. Whatever the case may be, create something that looks like any other Reddit post, something that blends in with the subreddits or other communities you wish to target.

Paid advertising is exciting and worth checking out. Make your ad campaign something that fits perfectly with whatever you want to do. A great campaign will include the best advertisements you can create while also standing out.

Chapter 47 – Tumblr

The next place to visit when marketing online through social media is Tumblr. This is a popular blogging platform that links people with the many things they love. Tumblr is more than just a regular blogging site. It is a place where people can display everything from pictures to videos and much more. It is one of the most diverse places to use online. People can exhibit everything from art pieces they have made to videos of their travels to different places.

Tumblr was created in 2007 as a microblogging site. It allows people to create short-form blog posts with multimedia features. A place focuses on things that people find interesting or what they are fans of. Tumblr focuses mainly on encouraging people to share what they love. By working with Tumblr, you could get people to love your company and brand.

What Do People Post on Tumblr?

Visit Tumblr, and you will find posts about everything from fashion and travel to movies and music. Some of the things people add onto their Tumblr pages include:

- Text posts to talk about trendy topics.

- Photos of things of interest; these include posts with multiple photos in a small album.

- Creative works of art; these include unique photos and art prints that people have created or even digital works of art.

- GIFs that display short videos of something fun; posts may include multiple GIFs that link together.

- Links to big news stories.

- Chats where people can list discussions. These include answers to anything someone posts on the Ask link.

- Audio files including streaming songs from Spotify etc.

- Videos; files from YouTube and Instagram can be shared on Tumblr.

Use all of these and more within your Tumblr marketing campaign. You can start a blog and write about anything you are selling. There are no limits to what you can post and share with others on Tumblr.

Who Uses Tumblr?

Tumblr is one of the youngest-skewing social media platforms around. In 2014 Business Insider established these statistics on Tumblr:

- Close to half of the people on Tumblr are in the 16-24 age range. Many of them use Tumblr to express themselves and the things they love.

- People in that age range also spend more time on Tumblr than they do on Twitter or Pinterest. The variety of posts people can find on Tumblr may be a big factor.

- About 35 million individuals use Tumblr in some form each month. Some people have their blogs on Tumblr. Others just forward things.

Tumblr is a wonderful place where people can get online and express their values and interests. Whether it is a video or audio file or just a simple link, share anything you want on Tumblr. You can get your photos posted on your Tumblr blog too. To make Tumblr worthwhile, know how to use it accurately.

Chapter 48 – Planning Your Tumblr Blog

You can create an outstanding Tumblr blog if you plan it right. Your Tumblr blog can include many attractive things related to your business. You need to generate a blog that expresses a memorable image people will associate with your work. It needs to be developed, so people know you are committed to using the site and that you want to reach them.

The best part of planning your Tumblr blog is that you can customize it in many ways.

1. Develop a strategy for your Tumblr blog.

Start working on your Tumblr blog by building an approach for using it. The strategy you use should include how you contact others on Tumblr. Consider the following points:

- Determine the types of posts you want to create. You can create posts to educate people about a topic or ones that interact with individual customers.

- Decide on the audience you wish to reach. Tumblr is best if you want to target a younger audience, but you should still look into other demographics based on interests, geographic location, and so forth.

- Use rich media content. It might be easier for people to read your work if you use pictures, videos etc within each of your posts.

2. Sign up for Tumblr and create a blog with a suitable name.

The name of the blog should be reflective of what you are promoting. The name could be the same as your business so people can easily find you on Tumblr, but that is optional.

3. Choose a user name that matches your business.

Your user name will be reflected in your Tumblr URL. People can enter your business name while writing your URL. For instance, a place named Joe's Coffee Shop could have a user name "joescoffeeshop," which would have the URL joescoffeeshop.tumblr.com. That user name is what people will see when they reblog your content, thus making it more visible.

4. Select a series of significant topics.

Tumblr will request that you enter at least five things that interest you. This would determine what you see on your dashboard. Ones that you like the most are prioritized. You can also disclose that your blog is associated with those key points. This lets other people on Tumblr see your blog before others.

Be careful of particular topics; only work with issues relevant to your business.

5. Choose a proper avatar and cover image for your blog.

The avatar will be displayed on a search engine. The cover image will show up at the top of your blog. They produce a memorable brand that illustrates your values.

6. Choose a theme your Tumblr page will feature.

A theme is a layout that organizes all the features on your Tumblr page. You have the option to use one of many pre-installed themes. A theme could include an outstanding template with a distinct color and font. It may also include boxes where specific bits of content will be found. You can always edit your theme later with certain fonts, colors, and other features that suit your image.

The general goal is to make your Tumblr posts visible on more searches and to get people to repost your work. You should still create an outstanding looking Tumblr blog to make your work more interesting. This helps to convey a visual brand.

Some Tumblr themes cost money. There are free options too, but those are not as unique or easy to adjust as the paid choices. Check tumblr.com/themes to see what is available.

7. Set up an About page.

The About page on your blog will have details on what your business offers. It can include additional contact information. Click the Customize Theme box on your dashboard to add the page.

You can also add an About box to the side of your blog that directly explains what your work is about. This box will appear on every post on your page.

8. Add a box on your Tumblr site that links people to your main business site.

Go to the Customize Theme section and add a box displaying a graphic listing of your website. This should be linked to the appropriate URL. The Customize Theme section will help you prepare a new box and URL in that spot. Watch for how the box looks; add a graphic that illustrates your brand if possible.

9. Add an Ask link. Go to the Edit Appearance part of your account and click the Ask option.

The Ask link allows people to ask you questions. It includes a box where someone on Tumblr can send a question or message to you. When you answer that question or remark you can share it on your blog. The person who inquired could potentially reblog your answer. This allows your knowledge of a topic to become easier for others to find.

The steps for setting up your own Tumblr blog are simple. After your blog is ready, start posting about your business and sharing content with others. This gets your word out to the younger audience that Tumblr targets.

Chapter 49 – Making Your Tumblr Blog Outstanding

Creating a Tumblr blog is easy. Using it to market you the right way is another thing. Use your Tumblr blog responsibly and with the right efforts to make what you have stand out. This chapter is about the many options to make your Tumblr experience outstanding.

How to Post Rich Media

The first thing to do when marketing on Tumblr is posting rich media on your page. Elegant media makes your posts more interesting. The odds of someone liking your posts will increase when you have a photo, GIF, video, or anything else of value on your page.

People are more likely to share your promotional content if it includes memorable pictures or videos. Rich media should be used to illustrate things like:

- Images of your products.

- Scenes of your work in action.

- Interesting tidbits or tips related to what you offer.

- Infographics that display many facts involving your field of work.

- Fun uses for anything you sell.

- Something that expresses how unique and distinct your business is.

This all works with a simple series of steps to use for adding your content.

1. Go to your main Tumblr page.

2. Click to add a new post.

3. Select from one of the different links on the menu.

You can add a GIF, photo, video, or audio file, among other things.

4. If you have something on your computer, upload it to Tumblr. The system lets you search through your computer to find a suitable file.

5. If you want to share an article from another site, enter the URL of that content.

6. Preview the media to see that it looks fine and plays back well.

7. Enter the description of the media.

Use Quality Tags

Tags are used on Tumblr same as the other social media platforms. The bottom part of the post is the box you will add content. There is a spot where you can insert these tags. These help people find your content through a search on Tumblr.

You can use the keywords and phrases you want in your content. But it is more important to add them as tags. The Tumblr search algorithm looks through tags first. This makes using tags in your Tumblr page all the more important.

To add tags:

1. Go to the foot of the post box once you finished.

2. Enter a series of keywords or phrases into the field.

3. Use a space between each keyword or phrase on each tag.

4. Adding a comma after each keyword or phrases will indicate that you are entering a hashtag.

5. Do this with as many tags as you wish.

Reblog Regularly

You can add new posts on your blog at any time. Your posts should reflect everything happening in your business. By adding more posts, you will get followers on Tumblr, thus increasing your overall reach. Even more importantly, Your followers are more likely to reblog your posts by putting them on their pages or by forwarding them to others who might be interested.

So, why not return the favor? Reblog other posts to show your interest. Your profile will appear in the Likes section of that post. This adds a new clickable link. Anyone who is interested will notice your Tumblr page.

The blog it came from automatically appears on a reblogged message. For instance, if you reblog something, the bottom of your post will include a link that goes where the blog originally appeared. It allows people on your page to go to that blog and learn what the original author offers.

The process is similar if any posts you create get reblogged. By getting more reblogs, links to your blog will be produced on other peoples' blogs. This makes your business even more visible because a larger audience has access to you. You have a better shot at getting more traffic on your Tumblr page if you promote your work well and get enough people to reblog what you post.

Reblogging not only helps you add content to your blog but also creates relationships. Post a reply message on something you reblog if you have a comment. That message will appear on the Likes section of the post, thus making your content stand out even more. Anything supportive of the original post or even something new that adds to its value is always a plus.

Solicit and Answer Asks

The first thing to do with Tumblr is to get people to ask questions on your blog. Tell people to click on the Ask box on your page to ask you questions relating to your business. Answer these questions clearly and promptly. People will rely on you when you answer and share good ideas of what makes your work outstanding and worthwhile.

Feel free to solicit asks. Allow people to ask questions about your business, your products, or anything related to your passion. Show them you understand the ins and outs of your line of work and genuinely want to help people find things of value.

Add Many Pages

You can also add individual pages on your Tumblr blog to highlight different things related to your business. A lawn care business can create one page devoted to landscaping and another to weed control, for example. Adding pages makes it easier finding content on your blog related to just one subject. Tumblr makes it trouble-free to add new pages:

1. Go to the Edit Appearance section of your page.

2. Click the Edit Theme option.

3. Select the Add a Page choice.

4. Enter details on the page including the name and description.

5. Select the URL that your page will link to. This could lead to a specific part of your Tumblr blog or to another social media site.

As mentioned in the prior chapter, use a larger and more visible section if you want to create a link to your official business website.

Share on Social Media

Tumblr has the option to link your updates on your site to a Facebook or Twitter account. To do this:

1. While working on a post, click the Facebook or Twitter logo at the bottom.

2. Enter the specific account you want to forward something.

3. Tumblr will format your content and display it on the appropriate feed. This also creates a link on your Facebook or Twitter page that leads directly to your Tumblr blog.

Sharing your work on social media will help people know that your business is on Tumblr. This also creates a new quality link to your social media page, thus making it easier to find.

A Note About the Layout

Regardless of how you use Tumblr to market yourself, look at the layout the site utilizes. The actual blog content will be organized in a vertical rectangle layout. This creates a display that can be read on both mobile and desktop devices. In other words, wide images and files laid out in a horizontal rectangle might be harder to read. Be aware of this when getting rich media content onto your site to view.

Chapter 50 – Can You Get Paid Ads on Tumblr? (It Might be Costly)

It is true you could buy paid advertisements on Tumblr. After all, many of the other social media sites you've read about here offer their own paid marketing options. Tumblr is no exception. However, there is a very serious hurdle you have to overcome just to get an ad set up.

The price tag that Tumblr charges for people to advertise is not humble. According to Business Insider, the minimum cost for an ad on Tumblr is $25,000. It is primarily due to how Tumblr has such a large base while focusing mainly on multimedia-based posts.

Tumblr also uses this $25,000 minimum as a means of keeping the Tumblr experience unique. People who spend that much money are generally more likely to have quality editing programs and dynamic sites. In other words, most small businesses would struggle to use paid advertising on Tumblr, let alone trying to create a dynamic ad memorable enough for people to want to click it. That does not mean they cannot try; it would just be a challenge to get noticed.

But If You Have the Money...

You can still get an advertisement on Tumblr provided you actually have the money for it. This process is clearly made with wealthier and more experienced businesses in mind. But a marketing routine is great if you have a large enough budget. It also works if you want to target the younger audience that Tumblr focuses on.

Here are some steps for making Tumblr's ad system work for you:

1. Go to tumblr.com/business to sign up for a business account.

The account may link up to the one you already have.

2. Go to your dashboard and either select a post you want to promote or create something new.

Tumblr gives you the option to work with either new or existing content.

3. Check the content you are using and see how it works for your campaign. You will not be able to edit any old content.

Watch for vibrant, rich media that displays your brand or anything important to you. People are more likely to respond to ads that look intriguing and have something valuable to say.

4. Preview your advertisement.

Tumblr ads are always prepared in a square format. The layout fits a basic video for playback on mobile devices. You don't have to use a video for your ad; Tumblr just uses this format for a display because so many advertisers use videos.

5. After getting your post ready, select the places you want to reach.

You can target your ads toward certain keywords and various demographics. These include demographics relating to location, age, and interests.

6. Enter your budget for how much you will spend for every click or a certain number of impressions. This includes how long the campaign will last.

As with any other social media platform, you have to spend more to make your work more visible. The minimum mentioned earlier is for a basic program that does not last too long. Your ad might be overwhelmed by ones who paid more for the service.

7. Click to place the ad.

Tumblr will review your ad and then let you know when it is available online. After this, use the analytics tool from the Tumblr business section to review how people are reacting.

The advertising support that Tumblr offers helps to get your words out to more places. A promoted post, whether it has new or existing content, will make your profile attractive and visible to more individuals.

Chapter 51 – Quora

Quora is different from many social media sites as it concentrates mainly on asking questions and getting answers. Use Quora to show people that you know a lot about your field of work.

Quora is a website that went online in 2010 after being created by a few former Facebook employees. The site was created for getting answers to complicated or detailed questions. It uses a Wikipedia-inspired design where people ask for information from the public.

How Quora Works

To know why Quora is great for your social media marketing, you have to know how Quora works:

1. Someone will go on Quora to ask a question.

The user will be as specific as possible when asking that question.

2. The inquisitor will post it in a section that is relevant to the subject.

There are many subsections on Quora were people can ask questions. These include sections for home improvement, auto maintenance, computer technology, entertainment, and many others. Quora maintains a very diverse layout of subsections.

3. Users on Quora respond to the question with their own answers.

The goal for each user is to describe the most detailed, creative, unique, and thoughtful answer. The response should have as much backup evidence or personal knowledge of the subjectas possible.

4. People then choose to upvote or downvote answers.

The answers with the most upvotes will appear above all others on the question page.

5. Visitors can also click the Interesting link on a question page to indicate that the issue or the conversation surrounding it is intriguing.

Questions that have more Interesting votes will appear above others on channels they were posted.

6. Comments can be included on individual answers. People may leave them to clarify data or to ask for additional points on what was listed.

Quora's main goal is twofold – it gives people answers to questions and triggers conversations about any topic. It creates a peaceful and interesting setup where people can talk to one another. The site proves that while there might be one very strong answer to a question, not everything has a definite answer.

So Why is This Important for Marketing?

Quora is essential for marketing as it is a place where you can show the world your knowledge. By answering questions on Quora, you let people know you have full comprehension of everything you market.

Quora is essential because it lets you share your experience. Let's say you run a craft brewery and want to let people know you understand the ins and outs of making beer. You could search for questions on Quora relating to craft beer and how to brew it. You can answer questions involving the right mix of water when preparing beer, how long the brewing cycle is, how to add flavor accents, and even storing beer while it matures.

Regardless of the field you work in, you can probably find questions worth answering on Quora. Just search to see what people are asking and what they need help with. By doing this, it becomes easy to make your mark and get people to see what you offer.

Chapter 52 – Using Quora Correctly

Quora is great when you want to show people how well you understand your line of work. By answering questions related to what your business does, people will see you as a trustworthy entity to do business with. It is easy to get onto Quora right now.

Signing Up

Signing up for Quora is simple:

1. Go to the Quora website at quora.com.

2. Enter your email address and a password.

3. Add your user name and other contact information. Keep the information as close to your business name as possible.

4. Select at least ten topics presented to you by Quora. The site does this to see what users are interested in.

5. Enter details on the topics you know about. Quora will display many topics you can select based on the options you enter in a search box.

Establishing a Profile

You need a profile on Quora to show users that you run a business and have the credentials to answer their questions. Here are some steps to use when creating your Quora profile:

1. Click your avatar to load your profile. You can edit the profile from here.

2. Upload a headshot of yourself. Use the most recent and best-quality image possible.

3. Enter your name.

4. Write your tagline of what you do. Do not directly list your business here.

Your name and tagline will appear on any answer you post.

5. Enter a description.

The description should include the following:

- What you do for a living.

- Specifics about how you work.

- A call-to-action at the end; this should include a link to your website.

Avoid directly mentioning the name of your business. The URL at the end is good enough. You can mention the business name in the next step.

6. Edit the Credentials and Highlights section.

Add details about:

- The business where you work.

- Your educational history.

- Where you currently live.

7. Enter your areas of expertise in the Knows About section.

You should have entered this while signing up for a Quora account. You can update this section to include more things you know about if you wish. Keep those points relevant to your business.

Answering Questions

Now that you have everything for your Quora account, start answering questions. Use these steps to answer anything:

1. Begin by looking at the individual Quora channels. You should have quick access to channels related to your interests and what you understand based on your profile.

2. Go to the search box at the top of the site to search for individual questions if you prefer to go that route.

3. Look for a question that you can answer.

4. Click the Answer button to write a response.

This will open a regular entry feature to write and format your answer in any way you see fit. You can add a photo, quote box, or link to your entry. The link would be best if you have an outside site other than yours that you might be referring to.

5. Submit your answer after you are finished writing.

This works best when you have a detailed and thoughtful answer. When you create something interesting and specific, your reader will notice that you fully understand and comprehend the content.

You will be competing with many others who answer the same question. Review the answers that people have posted, but see that your answer is more detailed and unique. Go into more specifics and be thorough when writing your response.

The answers that people like the most will be upvoted. The answer with the most upvotes is prominently displayed. Create a sensible and unique answer to improve your chances of having your answer upvoted.

Using Quora for marketing is easy. By answering questions relating to your market, people will see that you are an expert in your line of work. This will leadto more clicks on your profile and eventually visits to your business site. This is a smart form of social media marketing as you prove to your audience how clever and thoughtful you are.

Be careful with how you use Quora. The next chapter will look into the specific things to do when using Quora with marketing needs in mind.

Chapter 53 – Using Quora for Marketing

Your marketing campaign on Quora is all about showing that you understand certain concepts. Answer questions in a smart and sensible manner to show people that you and your business can be trusted. Quora lets you confirm that you understand your field of work. You can also prove to people on Quora that you care about others and hope to resolve any concerns people might have. This chapter includes important aspects of using Quora that must be followed to self-market the correct way.

Create a Great Profile

When you use Quora, you have to show the reader you have a clear idea of what you are talking about. They have to be convinced that you are a trustworthy person to notice. Do this by creating an outstanding profile.

Everything in your profile is displayed publicly. Add anything you can about yourself in the profile. Include a link to your site and talk about what you do for a living without sounding promotional. Tell people that you have an extensive amount of experience. Let them know that you are someone who really understands what you discuss and you want to share it.

Answer Correctly with Experience in Mind

Showing off your experience is a vital part of social media marketing. People are more likely to trust in others who have years of experience in their lines of work and are excited about what they offer. When you give an answer on Quora, show that experience to the reader. Talk about your knowledge and expertise in whatever you share.

Let the reader acknowledge you are referring to things you have done in the past. Let's go back to the craft beer example mentioned in this section of the book. When talking about brewing craft beer, you can talk about an experience trying to prepare a good lager. Explain how a lager beer is made and that you used a specific series of ingredients to make it. Clarify your experience and share your firsthand knowledge.

Be as Detailed as Possible

Having a lot of familiarity makes you more marketable on Quora. Being able to show that your knowledge is real is even more important. Give as many details as possible when producing an answer. You could even link a person to some website other than your own to validate your answer if needed. Don't forget to add photos if possible.

Try to produce a four- to six-paragraph answer to the question. Respond to it in many parts and look into the various considerations that might be of influence. For the craft beer example, you could answer a question about the right conditions for brewing beer by going into the many aspects of the brewing process. You could talk about how the conditions for growing hops are different from the ideal temperature that a beer vat is kept.

Show the reader that you understand and write a heavily detailed reply. Being as specific and direct as possible is vital to your Quora success.

Avoid Trying to Drive Traffic

As with Reddit, avoid being too promotional when writing things on Quora. The site disapproves of users who write answers designed to bring traffic elsewhere. An answer that appears to be an obvious marketing post will be flagged by

Quora as spam. You could be booted off if you try to drive traffic to your page.

Do not add a link to your website in your answers. No specific details of what your business does either. Only list what you feel is appropriate when talking about your experience without referring to your specific business or other things you have done. Being sensible when talking about your work is essential to your success. This means not sounding like you want someone's business. Besides, Quora would be despondent if you blatantly tried to market yourself like that.

Chapter 54 – Periscope

Do you want to market yourself with live events where people can join and see what you are doing in real time? Periscope is the social media choice for you. You have read earlier about how Facebook and YouTube allow you to have live streams to record things and interact with people in real time. Well, Periscope is a social media platform that is fully dedicated to live streaming activities.

Periscope is a video-streaming program that can be used on desktop computers and mobile devices. It was created in 2015 and was acquired by Twitter not long before it opened. The concept was to make it easier for people to see things from all around the world. The founder got the idea for Periscope in 2013 after reading about the Taksim Square protests in Istanbul. He was able to read about the protests but wanted to see them to get an idea of how enormous they were.

This led to the creation of Periscope. It was designed with the intention of letting people broadcast themselves from anywhere in the world. Whether it was traveling to some unique location or being in the middle of a major news story, Periscope lets people record themselves in real time and stream what they are doing to other people. This gives everyone the opportunity to see something special and dynamic.

How it Works

Periscope uses a simple setup:

1. Download the app and sign up for an account. Periscope is free for people who sign up to use.

2. Set up a live streaming event. This could be a description of the event and some tags to let people know what it is about.

3. Tap on the record feature on your camera to get it to work. This lets you start the show.

This is a simple approach to marketing yourself that you are bound to love playing with. When using Periscope, you will have full control over all the things you want to say or do on the site. Look at this option when wanting something fun to promote your work with.

Why Use Periscope?

You can use Periscope to make your business easier for people to find online. There are many good reasons why Periscope is valuable:

- It gives you richer content to work with. The live streaming content that Periscope supports gives people access to amazing events.

- Your Periscope posts will feel a little more urgent than other traditional social media posts because you are getting things out to people right now in a vibrant manner.

- You can get in touch with your customers by using Periscope. The program lets you interact with people while the stream is happening.

- People who are curious about a certain subject might come across your events while searching through their favorite tags. You might be surprised at who will get onto your streams.

- It also offers a simple layout where people can play back your stream at any time. You can get your live stream online even after it is over.

Use it Carefully

As with any other video-streaming function, watch how you are using Periscope. Avoid using it to record copyrighted events. It is illegal and can lead to significant trouble through fines or imprisonment.

There have been many cases where people have abused Periscope's abilities. An example is that numerous people used Periscope to stream episodes of the television series Game of Thrones to others who do not have access to the channel. In this case, anyone who is streaming a show like this is breaking the law. Something that people should be paying for is getting out to the public free of charge.

Avoid being involved in such activities. Use Periscope to stream events that are available to the public. Periscope is popular with individuals who do not have traditional access to public events for whatever reason.

Chapter 55 – Running a Quality Periscope Session

Plan a sensible intention for using Periscope before you start your event. This objective could be anything relating to how well Periscope can be run. There are many things you can do on Periscope to have fun and get in touch.

Demonstrate Products

The first idea for using Periscope is to demonstrate products or services you offer. On Periscope, you can stream a customer using something you have for sale. A person could taste a new meal available at a restaurant or sport some fashions a boutique is selling. A live demonstration lets people know what to expect from your work. People will trust your business if they see what your product or service is like in action on Periscope.

Hold a Special Meeting

Periscope is great when you want to hold a meeting with others. Create an open meeting where people can chat with you about what's happening in your business. In return, tell people about your business plans and what you want to offer in the future. You can hold such a meeting to let people know what you are doing and how your efforts work. Think of a Periscope session as an open house where you are ready to tell people anything and then answer questions in return.

Show People What Happens in Your Workplace

You can also take Periscope to an event that takes place where you work. You could bring your smart device into a convention event, a board meeting, or any other special event that is happening. You can even bring your device out on your sales floor if you have one just to let people see what is happening. This could be used to invite people to your store. Let viewers see what you are doing in real time, and they will have an interest in doing business with you.

Solicit Information

You can always get information from people who want to get onto your Periscope stream. Do this by asking people to send their email addresses to access your event. With this, you can adjust the settings on your Periscope event so only people with certain email addresses can see it. This lets you add to your mailing list for marketing. Be advised that you will have to enter those email addresses for your event manually. You might need assistance if you have many addresses.

Can You Follow People Too?

You have the option to follow different sessions on Periscope if you wish. You can get onto another person's Periscope stream and leave insightful comments about that person's work on the stream. This is great if you want to talk with someone and share your knowledge. People could even click your profile and learn more about you and your business when they see what you do. Those people might be intrigued by what you have to say.

Chapter 56 – Using Periscope Correctly

Marketing with Periscope is easy when you get it running correctly. Several things will go into play as you plan your Periscope sessions with other people.

Sign Up With the Right Group

First, you have to sign up with a proper social media account. This is best as it links your Periscope streams with your social media page.

1. Go to the Create New Account section.

2. Tap the Facebook, Twitter, or Google Plus option.

3. Log onto your account with the appropriate social media site.

4. Your profile data from the social media site will be imported to your Periscope account. You can make a few adjustments to the layout as you see fit.

5. Enter your name and a handle. You can use a handle different from your regular Twitter or Facebook handle if desired.

This is important for marketing as it creates a consistent brand. You could always announce on Facebook that you will be on Periscope at a certain time, for instance. Then log onto Periscope with your Facebook account. Your data on the Periscope profile will be identical to what is on Facebook.

Connect an Account

What's even more important for marketing is to make your Periscope streams more visible on other social media sites. Not all people are aware of what Periscope has to offer. By posting your streams on Facebook or another popular space you might be active on, people will promptly see what you offer.

1. Go to your profile.

2. Visit the Connected Accounts section.

3. Tap a link to connect your profile to specific platforms.

4. Log into the profile in question.

5. Confirm the link between Periscope and the Facebook or Twitter account you are setting up.

Get Verified (Via Twitter)

You should also be verified on Periscope. People who notice that you are verified will trust your work and watch it. More importantly, people will take you seriously because you have put in the effort to get verified in the first place.

Periscope does not actually help you get verified. Rather, you need to get a Twitter account to be verified. When you link your Periscope account to a verified Twitter feed, your Periscope page will have that blue mark saying you are verified. Refer to the Twitter section of this book to see how to get verified through that site.

Getting a Great Stream Ready

Now that you are set on Periscope, you can create your streaming event. The steps to use for getting the stream up and running are easy to follow.

1. Start by marketing on other social media accounts or on your website as to when you will be on Periscope.

Let people know as soon as possible when you will be streaming on Periscope and why you are doing it. You could always leave your stream available after it is over, but letting people know ahead of time is best. This is to let them interact with you directly.

2. Open Periscope on your device and tap the proper button.

The Android version uses a Camera button. The iOS version has a Broadcast tab.

3. Enter the name of the event.

The event name should be reflective of what you are doing. It can include your business name and maybe a description of what the event is about. It could be some occasion you are taking part in, for instance. The name could also reflect whatever you want to discuss. Remember, people can search for your event through a search bar on the top of the Periscope app or site.

4. Enter tags for your event.

Tags are needed to help people find your event on Periscope. People can even click one of the tagged channels on Periscope to easily find your work. Use a tag that relates to one of the major Periscope channels like #inspire, #talk, #food, #music, #sports, or #travel, among others. Use something relevant to your work; try to incorporate two or three of these tags if possible.

5. Determine whom you will share the event with.

You can make the event public if desired. You could also create a private group where only people with certain email addresses can access it.

6. Check the private group you want to utilize. Create a group by selecting the proper option on the screen and

by entering the specific info on each person who can have access.

You should use the email addresses that you might have solicited from persons who wanted to join your group as mentioned in the last chapter. Get your group set up well before the event just to be safe. After all, you might have many addresses to work with when getting everything in order.

7. Share your location if desired. Click the arrow button to let your device review your location or enter a custom one.

This is important if you want people to know where you are. It is great for local business marketing, as your feed will appear on peoples' devices or browsers if they are near you.

8. Tap the Twitter icon to broadcast an announcement that your event will start soon.

You need to keep your Periscope account linked to your Twitter feed to use this. Also, if you use this, try to keep the name of your event short. The event name will be listed in the tweet being sent. It could be cut off if the title is too long.

9. Tap the option to go live.

Now you can get your event is running. Use this to interact with people in any way you see fit. The prior chapter reviews how to use Periscope for marketing.

10. Swipe the screen on your device down when you are finished with the event. Tap the button to stop the broadcast at this point.

11. You can also keep the stream active for as long as you want. You can delete it from your account later on if necessary.

People cannot leave comments or feedback when watching a previously recorded stream. They can still share those streams with others on Facebook or Twitter or by copying a link to the stream. Additionally, people can move from one end of the stream to the other as desired.

Watch How People Interact

Watch how people interact with you while your Periscope event is running. Here are some steps to review what is happening with your Periscope event:

1. Check the number next to the Live icon.

The number shows how many people are on your stream at a given time.

2. Look at the heart signs on the screen.

When people like what you are doing, they will tap the heart symbol on the screen. This causes a heart to rise up over the screen. This shows that someone likes what you are doing. Watch for how these hearts come in different colors too; the more colors the more unique users like your work.

3. Check the chat feature on the side of the screen.

People can chat with you during your stream.

4. Answer any comments people are leaving.

As mentioned earlier, always respond. Address the person leaving a message by name.

Watch how people interact with you during your Periscope session. See that they are getting in touch with you consistently and that everything is running well. Being in direct contact with people during your session is important.

Periscope is perfect when you're looking to share things with other people. Make sure you look at how well Periscope is used, so it isn't going to be hard to handle. It is easy to get the most out of your live streams.

Chapter 57 – Goodreads

Do you have a book you want to sell? You might have a book designed to illustrate your expertise in a certain field related to your business. A landscaping professional might publish a book about preparing a landscape on one's property. The professional could use this to market his or her knowledge of how to handle landscaping tasks. This could lead to people using that person's services because they see the landscaper trustworthy.

How would someone present that book to other people? That individual could promote the book through Goodreads.

On the surface, Goodreads appears to be a place where you would share book recommendations. This is popular given that the literature world is diverse and full of unique and entertaining stories. Goodreads is also a place to market your business. The site does well for those who have publications they want to share.

Goodreads is a popular site that has been operating since 2006. It is served by Amazon and is a place to find information on books of all sorts. People on the site can:

- Review books

- Give their own suggestions for books

- Discuss various books

- Create blog posts to talk about literature

- Participate in polls relating to books

Goodreads has been growing in size since it was formed. It currently has more than 60 million users and cataloguing hundreds of millions of books.

What does Goodreads offer for your marketing? With Goodreads, you can promote a book you have written. You can use Goodreads to also market any digital books you created in conjunction with your business. You can also use the blog features and recommendations on Goodreads to help you highlight books based on your interests including your business.

You can even have people buy your book through Goodreads. The Amazon link on Goodreads ensures your book is listed on Goodreads and on Amazon as well. This service is great for independent authors who want to expose their works to the public.

How to Use Goodreads

There are many ways how you can benefit from using Goodreads:

- Start up an author page that includes all the details of what you do and how you can offer something of value to people who read your work.

- Share what you have been reading through Goodreads. Create virtual shelves that contain the books you are reading or have read.

- Hold discussions with others on Goodreads. Q&A sessions relating to books you have written could be held through the site.

- Start up a blog that highlights your writing. Write about what interests you and the work you do.

Goodreads is an ideal place for marketing if you ever want to highlight your books. You can get Goodreads to work to your advantage.

Chapter 58 – Working With Goodreads

Know what you can do when getting Goodreads ready for your social media marketing requirements. You can always sign up for a standard account to create listings of your favorite books and leave reviews.

Create a Detailed Profile

Start working with Goodreads by using a detailed profile. It is easy to sign up for a profile with Goodreads:

1. Begin by adding an avatar photo. This should be a recent photo of you.

2. Enter a biography about who you are and what you do. Don't be overly promotional. Add a URL where people can learn more about you. This URL should be a link to your business site.

3. Add social media reference sites to your profile too. List as many social media sites for your business as possible.

4. Add a number of your favorite books to your account. You can add details in your profile about the books that are your favorites. Include at least ten books relating to your line of work by searching based on title or ISBN.

Rate and Comment on Books

After signing up, you can start using Goodreads to rate certain books of interest to you. You can move throughout Goodreads to find books in any genre:

1. Search for the book you want to comment on.

2. Click the green button stating that you either want to read a book, that you are currently reading it, or that you have finished reading it.

3. Click the particular star rating you want to give to that book.

4. Add a comment about the book if you are inclined. The note should be detailed and honest.

Create a Bookshelf

A Bookshelf is perfect for your account. This is where you organize a series of books that interest you. It can be reviewed by anyone.

1. Go to the page for a book you want to add to a shelf.

2. Click the Want to Read option to place the book on your to-read shelf. You can also move the book to a shelf of books you are currently reading by confirming on that same menu that you are reading it right now.

3. While on your account, check and update your Currently Reading section when you have finished reading a book. Click to indicate that you have read the book.

4. Go to the My Books section of your account to add a shelf. Click the edit link to add a new shelf. This could be anything relating to books in certain categories or fields of work.

Ask Questions

You should ask questions to writers who are on Goodreads. Asking questions of a writer in your field of work is perfect.

1. Go to the page for a particular writer.

2. Click on the book of that writer.

3. Go to the Reader Q&A section on the book entry.

4. Ask the author a thoughtful question.

You can always mention you have experience in a field and you want to get confirmation about something. Indicate that you have knowledge of the field the book is about so the author will pay attention to you.

5. After the author provides an answer (if applicable), acknowledge this and thank them. You could also ask a follow-up question if you want.

Chapter 59 – Using Goodreads As an Author

Do you have a book you have had published? You can quickly set up an author account with Goodreads. An author account lets you promote your book and interact with other people in any way you see fit. You can use this to market your work and to encourage people to check out any books you have written. Goodreads works well if you have published books in conjunction with your main work; you will not only promote your books but also what you do for a living.

Submit a Book to Amazon

Any book you have written must be submitted to Amazon before you can get an author profile:

1. Log onto Amazon or sign up for an Amazon account.

2. Go to kdp.amazon.com while logged in. This brings you to the Kindle Direct Publishing site; this is where people can submit books for sale.

3. Go to the Bookshelf section.

4. Create a new title in the Bookshelf. Choose to enter a Kindle eBook; this is what Amazon requests you use.

5. Enter details on the content of the book. Add relevant keywords and categories to be used for your book to be listed.

6. Add a cover for the book to be identified.

7. List the pricing plan you have for the book if desired. You should also list where you have distribution rights for the book if needed.

Starting an Account

After getting your book on Goodreads, you can log onto the site and get listed as an author.

To apply for an author account:

1. Sign in to your Goodreads account.

2. Enter the title of your book, the ISBN or other identifying points.

3. Click the author profile page. Look for the Is This You button and click it.

4. Fill out the proper form. You might have to scan a proof of identity.

5. You will receive an email in about two business days confirming your new author account. The login information for your account will not change.

With this, you will now have access to all the main Q&A functions and other review points that a book listing has.

Answer Peoples' Questions

A great way to promote your work as an author is to answer questions people have. This lets people see that you are knowledgeable about your field.

1. Go to your profile page or any page for a book you have listed.

2. Check on any questions people have left on your page.

3. Answer the questions as soon as possible. Be thoughtful and appreciative of what people are asking. Be prompt too.

Work With a Blog

You can produce your own Goodreads blog for people to learn about your work as well. Share your inspiration with others and present information about what you want to highlight. This will work perfectly if your book is linked to your business. Your blog could bridge some connections between your business and what you have written.

1. Go onto your main profile page.

2. Click on the blog section.

3. Enter a new post as you see fit. Make it something relating to your work and your interests.

4. You can also add pictures or other bits of content. Keep that content relevant to the book.

Get Paid Ads

As an author, you can also get paid ads on Goodreads. Paid advertisements help people be aware of your work. Use this if you have a new book that you want to promote.

1. Go to goodreads.com/advertisers to get started. Make sure you are logged in.

2. Enter details on the book you wish to promote. The book must be listed on the website.

3. Enter details about where to present your ads.

Your ads will automatically appear on one of the ad display features on the site. You can configure where the ad will be featured based on your target audience. You can reach people according to genre, location, or age, among other things. Don't forget to list the keywords you want to target.

4. Determine how much you want to spend on your campaign during its lifespan or your daily budget.

It costs 50 cents per click to use the advertising system. This is a set price.

5. The analytics feature from Goodreads will disclose how many people are clicking and viewing your ad. Use this to see how many people are buying your book thanks to your ad.

Goodreads is great if you are trying to promote your work as a writer. You could use it to highlight any books you have written; particularly ones that relate to a larger business you are working with. Look at how Goodreads can be useful for your marketing today; you will see that it is more valuable than you think.

Chapter 60 – Flickr

The last of the social media sites we will talk about is Flickr. This is a website that hosts photos. It is operated by Yahoo. Flickr is an attractive website for photos, but it is also a place advertisers use to reach the public.

Flickr was created in 2004 to host photos files. The business was acquired by Yahoo a year later. Flickr evolved to include apps for most mobile devices plus a browser website optimized for tablets. It is estimated that there are around 50 million registered Flickr users with about 25 million active users. Flickr also estimates that people spend about three to six minutes on the site on average after loading it up. There are billions of photos on Flickr.

An important part of Flickr is that it is a more professional spot for photography than other places you have read about in this guide. The site focuses extensively on professional-quality shots. These include photos taken with only the finest high-definition cameras. Flickr is perfect for people who love photography and want to find the highest-quality shots.

What Can You Promote on Flickr?

With Flickr, you can take pictures of anything relating to your business, such as:

- Your business location.

- Any products you offer.

- People utilizing the products you sell.

- Things that might have inspired your work.

- Photos relating to the history of your business.

Why Use Flickr?

While a site that focuses on just photos might not sound like something for your marketing, you could actually use Flickr for many marketing ideas. Some options are:

- List some of your own photos that only you can use. You can create permission requirements for those images.

Permissions would require people to ask for consent to use any photos you have. This ensures your business name will be spread to places where your photos are being used, but only the photos that you want people to share.

- You can also add inbound links. Each photo you take can include a link to your website.

- Photos also illustrate in clear detail what you are selling and your business.

- More importantly, Flickr gives you the chance to tell people your story. It lets you share what motivates you and what influences shaped your business.

Chapter 61 – How to Use Flickr

The good news is that it only takes a few moments to get online and get your content moved to Flickr. You might have to edit your photos depending on how they appear, see that your photos are available for display.

Signing Up

Flickr is free to sign up. You just need a Yahoo account to get started:

1. Log on to a Yahoo email account. You might have to create one.

2. Enter your screen name.

3. Go to the Settings menu on your account to adjust your profile. The profile needs to be as detailed as possible.

You will get an account that offers one terabyte of photo storage. You can also use various editing tools on Flickr with your account. You could pay extra to get a Pro account, although that is optional. A Pro account provides you with ad-free possibilities.

Use a Professional Camera

When taking pictures for Flickr it is vital that you use a high-quality professional camera. This will help you take beautiful photos that can be expanded in size or edited in many ways. The photo files you upload could include meta data that lists info on the camera that was used, the settings used to take the photo, and so forth. This content can be included in your photo listing to create a sense of formality within your page. You would also need a memory card to save the images or a link that connects your camera to your computer.

Uploading Content

After you get on Flickr with your top-quality camera ready, you can upload content onto the site:

1. Click on the appropriate upload button.

2. Connect your photo storage card or camera to your computer.

3. Select the photo from your camera.

4. Add a description and title.

The title and description should be as distinct and precise as possible. Use relevant keywords while explaining the back-story of your work.

5. Add a proper URL to your site in your description. This is to create the inbound link your site requires.

Mention how people can go to that site to learn more about your photo. Do not make the content look or feel overly promotional.

6. Add some tags to the photo.

You can use as many tags as you wish. Make them specific and rational.

7. Add your photos to an album.

Create an album with a unique title and description. Use as many albums as you want, but always add each photo you take to the appropriate album.

8. Choose the group where you want to add your photo.

9. Select the proper license for your photo.

10. Upload.

Get into Groups

While on Flickr, look for groups that you might be interested in. Groups are people posting photos about the same concept. Adding your work into groups is fun and easy to do. Use your photos to your group that you have interest in what they are about. This leads people to see your profile and eventually get onto your website.

1. Click on the search bar at the top of the Flickr site.

2. Enter a keyword.

3. Click the option to search for groups with that keyword.

4. Review each group based on the photos it has, who contributes, and what the rules of use are.

5. Click the Join button to enter a group.

6. Afterwards, collect individual photos in your account. Select the option on each photo to add to a group.

Getting a License Ready

A critical part of using Flickr involves getting an appropriate license. A license refers to how people can use your images. When uploading a photo, you can choose the license options. Decide the proper one so you can get credit. Thanks to the links produced by some licenses, this could help make your site more visible.

Attribution

The Attribution license option is the best for marketing. With an Attribution license, people will have the right to display and share your photo. However, the person sending it must give you full credit for the photo. This should have a link back to your Flickr page or website. You can set individual rules on the Attribution license within your photo's description.

Public Domain

Your photo can also be listed in the public domain. This means a person people can share the photo in any way they want without copyright restrictions. This is appropriate if you have a photo that you feel can be shared anywhere. By releasing this in the public domain, you are foregoing any reference or legal rights to the photo. You can use it for your own needs, but anyone else can do the same.

Noncommercial

Another license option is to let people distribute your photo for noncommercial purposes. People can send your photo anywhere provided it is not for financial gain. The only person who should be using the photo for commercial gain at this point is you.

Setting Permissions

You can get permissions set up for who can use your photos. This ensures that certain photos you take can be shared with others online:

1. Go to your Settings menu.

2. Click on the Privacy and Permissions tab.

3. Edit options over who can download your images.

4. Specify if you want people to share your photos with others.

Sharing Photos on Other Social Media Sites

Your Flickr photos can go onto your other social media sites. You can use this if you have photos that you want to share with your business profiles as a means of marketing your work:

1. Go to your personal Settings.

2. Click on the Sharing and Extending tab.

3. Click the Connect button to link a Flickr account to a Tumblr, Twitter, or Facebook account.

4. Log into the account.

Make sure that you share your photos with accounts relevant to your business.

Editing Your Photos

You have the option to edit your photos on Flickr. You can use many controls to make the most of your photos:

1. Click on a photo you want to edit.

2. Go to the proper edit button on the photo page to open the Flickr Photo Editor.

3. Choose how you want to adjust the photo.

The things you can do include:

- Cropping items out of a photo, you can create a 4:3 or 16:9 layout for a photo here.

- Add filters to change how colors are displayed.

- Insert text into any spot on the photo.

- Use stickers or paint brushes to add whimsical touches.

- Use selective blur features to censor faces, identifying numbers, and other things you want to keep from being visible.

- Add a frame around the photo.

4. Click the Save button when you are finished.

Use Comments

Whenever you can don't forget to leave comments on Flickr. By adding comments, you let people on Flickr know what you think about their photos. Each comment includes a link to your profile that contains links to your website and Flickr page. Keep your comments insightful and friendly. This could lead people to your page where they could leave comments for you. (Don't forget to respond to those comments.)

Working with Flickr is great. Flickr lets you promote yourself in a visually stunning technique. The photos you take can be very detailed and brilliant and could help you spread the word. Make sure you take first-class photos and use the right camera. Also, make sure you edit your photos as needed.

Conclusion

This book has covered all the major social media platforms available to market your work online. It is hoped that you learned about with the benefits of social media and how to make it work to your advantage.

The amazing thing is that social media is a diverse landscape. Every social media site is different due to the clientele or of the layout of the pages. Perhaps it is about how people send messages to each other. Even the atmosphere, whether it is formal or informal, can make a difference.

No matter what platform you choose, one thing is certain. Social media is truly a dynamic concept that is always evolving and changing with the times. There are always going to be new options for social media and plenty of great features on each of these sites.

It only makes sense that you take advantage of all these platforms to market your business. Social media marketing is all about getting people to see what you have to offer. It is about getting people to hear you. More importantly, social media encourages great conversations and can establish powerful friendships.

Be sure to use the points in this guide to help you make the most out of any social media you prefer. Always follow the instructions and use common sense to create great posts or advertisements. What you have learned will steer you toward the right moves and decisions as you go online and have fun.

Preview of "Affiliate Marketing" by Noah Gray

Chapter 1 – What Is Affiliate Marketing?

Affiliate marketing has become popular over the years. It is estimated that the affiliate marketing industry in the United States is worth nearly $5 billion a year and brands in the United Kingdom are worth £1 billion. In addition, more than three-quarters of brands use some form of affiliate marketing to promote their products.

The types of businesses that are utilizing affiliate marketing are diverse in nature. You will find health care product companies, travel agencies, fashion brands, and many others working with these campaigns. Practically any business in the world can start using affiliate marketing if enough ideas are produced.

What is affiliate marketing and what makes it such a popular option for making money? This chapter is about what makes this practice unique and noteworthy. Affiliate marketing is a practice where a person promotes a business and receives money from that business for each sale or referral. It is a simple way of making money online.

This is a growing market and much of its popularity is due to how the process works, and how it makes it easier for people to promote what they are offering to others in a simple and easy-to-follow way.

The Main Definition

Affiliate marketing is a practice that can take many forms although it is particularly popular online. With this form of marketing, a business will entrust its promotional efforts to others. This practice works with a simple setup. A company allows people who sign up as marketers to promote their business and/or products. A company will offer particular referral codes and promotional materials to those marketers.

A marketer then offers the products and/or materials online. This can be done on a personalized website or blog, among other places. The key is that these promotional materials have to be visible. Visitors to a site will then click on a link that the affiliate has posted online. The visitor must reach a site through that particular link before the affiliate can be paid anything.

Affiliates will receive a small cut of the sales that are driven by their work. The total will vary based on where the affiliate goes for the campaign. If the campaign works well, it can be a great way to earn money.

Why Is This Useful for a Business?

Affiliate marketing is a way to make money from home that can benefit anyone. It is a simple process that helps merchants to get their products and services out to a larger audience. It also allows merchants to keep the pressure of marketing from being too intense. This occurs because companies are allowing the public to market their wares.

By letting affiliates market products, a merchant can more easily focus on production, rather than marketing. This can also give a brand the opportunity to be promoted in a variety of ways. While any company could put up web advertisements or even promote itself on television, sometimes those messages become too repetitive. They can get so old that they will lose their meaning. For instance, all those ads for car insurance that you watch on television could become so repetitive that you no longer really care that a particular insurance provider might promise you better deals on a policy.

However, with affiliate marketing, a business can be promoted with a greater variety of messages. Each affiliate could market a product with his or her own particular messages. These might involve reviews, demonstrations, or news stories about whatever is available.

A business will appreciate the affiliate marketing process as it allows the marketing to be a little more exciting. Use your own creativity and consider many ideas you might have to promote a product or company.

The Main Players

There are several people who must work together to make any affiliate marketing campaign effective. These people are the following:

The Merchant

The merchant is the business responsible for starting up the affiliate marketing campaign. The merchant may also be called the business, retailer, advertiser, or brand. The merchant sells a certain product or service. It could sell tangible products for use in the home or business. It could also sell travel services, financial solutions, broadband online access, or anything else that people spend money on. A merchant must initiate a campaign. The merchant will set up the rules about how the campaign is to be run and how people are to be compensated.

The Network

While you can find many merchants with whom to do business, you need to contact a merchant through a particular network. This is to make it easier for you to find something available for your use. The network is the grouping that offers an affiliate program in which people can participate. The network works with the merchant, in that the party who wants to be an affiliate will have to prepare a reasonable campaign and list it on the network site.

When the affiliate finds the marketing opportunity, the network will send information to the merchant regarding who has signed up. The merchant then sends out the proper marketing materials for the task at hand. The network also helps with managing the payments that take place during the campaign. It reviews how well affiliates work and delivers money based on what an affiliate can do.

A network will also receive some of the profits from each sale. These are not necessarily worth as much as what the affiliate or the merchant will receive but can still be worthwhile. In some cases, the network might provide the merchant with templates for the marketing materials to be utilized. Such templates can vary according to each network but they should be easy to customize and then implement. You do not always have to go through a network when finding a marketing campaign but it does help to at least get the support of one.

The Affiliate

Your role in the chain is as an affiliate. It is your work that is vital to the success of any marketing effort. The affiliate is the person who is responsible for getting the word out on whatever the merchant is offering. The affiliate will sign up with the merchant's plan through a network.

The affiliate can be anyone. It could be a blogger, a website operator, or a social media maven. Whatever the case, the affiliate should be someone who can get around online and interact with people in many ways. This person will accept information about all the materials that the merchant offers through the network. The affiliate will then have to manage the marketing items and use them properly as a means of potentially receiving a good payout.

In some cases, a separate manager can help with operating the affiliate program. This might entail working with a website or another method of promotion on a regular basis. Either way, monitoring and a lot of effort are required to ensure that the marketing process works well.

The Customer

The customer is the fourth and most important part of the affiliate marketing process. Without the customer, the campaign in question will fail. The marketing materials must reach the customer for the campaign to be successful. The affiliate must make sure such marketing items are appealing and useful in the eyes of the potential client. This ensures that the client will feel motivated and willing to become a customer.

With all four parties working together in the affiliate marketing process, it becomes easier for each of them to get what they want. Merchants can get the word out about their products and are more likely to make money. Networks can help with forwarding offers to the public and even participate in the profits. Affiliates will earn money from each referral that they produce. Finally, customers benefit by having access to information on a product or service that they are interested in and wish to purchase.

The customer is the key to ensuring that the marketing campaign works. Plenty of effort is needed by the other three parties to create messages and products or services that are worthwhile and of interest but in the end it is up to the customer to decide if a transaction is made.

In particular:

1. The merchant must have a useful product.

2. The network must be able to establish a platform for the merchant to use.

3. The affiliate has to create a smart campaign that is unique and works to highlight what the merchant is selling.

The true magic happens when all three parties work together.

A General Layout for Bringing in Payouts

Here's how affiliate marketing works:

1. A merchant will contact a network to solicit help with producing a new campaign.

2. The network informs the merchant what promotional materials are needed.

3. The merchant configures the promotional materials with messages and images that fit whatever is being offered.

4. An affiliate signs up to work with the merchant to promote the products.

5. The affiliate will utilize the materials that he/she has received from the merchant to initiate a campaign designed by the affiliate.

6. A website, blog, or other places that list these advertisements or other messages are investigated and chosen by the affiliate. The affiliate will then program the marketing materials properly while consistently updating and controlling the materials.

7. A customer will click on a link or advertisement on such a website or blog.

8. The customer will have a cookie stored on the network's browser which indicates that he or she was referred to a site by the affiliate.

9. The customer purchases a product on the website to which he or she was led by the affiliate. The cookie that lists the referral information may be intact for a period of time.

10. The affiliate will receive a portion of the sale that was produced. This is an amount or percentage predetermined by the merchant,

11. The network also receives a portion of the sale.

This is a very simple layout to follow and provides a person with earnings from each sale that takes place. The process also shows just how important all four parties are in the process. All parties must work together to ensure that a transaction can be accomplished effectively.

How Cookies Fit in

A major part of getting an affiliate marketing campaign to work is getting technology to play its part. The main technological element is the use of cookies. Cookies are necessary to identify the parties that cause sales to take place. Without them, it becomes impossible for a merchant to offer a marketing campaign to the public.

A cookie is an essential component of the marketing process. A cookie is placed on a web browser and stores information based on a person's user preferences, login information, and shopping cart contents, as well as other information. Cookies allow a browser to remember what a person is doing when online. They are also used by websites to tailor their messages to users.

Have you ever gone to a website and then noticed lots of ads for it on other sites shortly after? This is because cookies on your browser are listing details of what you have been doing while online. Those cookies have saved information about what sites you visited online.

This is relevant to the marketing campaign as a cookie remembers that a user entered a site through a link that was produced by the merchant and sent out to the public by an affiliate. The cookie has information on which affiliate was specifically responsible for getting the advertisement up and running.

Cookies work in the affiliate marketing process with a distinct setup. A cookie will remember the link that a person used to access a site. In this form of marketing, a first-party cookie is used. When customers click on a link from an affiliate, they will have a tracking cookie placed onto their browser. This first-party cookie lists information about:

- the advertiser.

- the affiliate.

- a network that everything links up.

- the commission total involved.

This cookie lists information on who will be paid in the event the customer makes a successful transaction. How long the cookie lasts will vary based on where it comes from. This is a special point about affiliate marketing that makes it worthwhile. You can get more money from your sales when you get access to cookies that are easy to support.

What Can Be Promoted?

Practically anything can be promoted for sale through an affiliate marketing campaign. Some of the products and services you can promote online are listed below.

- The health care industry is a big driver of the affiliate marketing industry. People often promote prominent supplements, services, and health goods online.

- Books about all kinds of subjects are promoted online too. These include recipe books, weight loss guides, and even books on how to take care of specific types of pets.

- Computer software can be promoted through a campaign. You could use your campaign to highlight any kind of program that people could download or purchase online.

- Travel services are big in the affiliate marketing industry. These include services like air travel, hotel services, or booking solutions.

- Tech products are always being marketed online through affiliate programs. These tech products include tablets and smartphones, portable media players, television sets, and smart appliances.

- The auto industry can benefit from affiliate marketing too. Companies that make car products like floor mats, cargo materials, electronic adapters, assorted parts, tires, shocks, or brakes can look to affiliates to help get their campaigns off the ground.

There are no real limits on what people can promote through affiliate marketing campaigns. You have the option to market anything you want although the marketing options you have to work with will vary based on where you go to find them. Search diligently to see what you could utilize to find a campaign worth promoting.

How to Find Opportunities

It is easy to find affiliate marketing opportunities today. You can go online and find a program directory or a network website that lists information on what is available. You can also go directly to the website of a merchant who is running a program. You can get specific information on that site about what is available to use.

The options available to you when finding marketing campaigns are vast. Search to see what is open and you will surely find something that interests you. Check on a search engine to see what is out there.

How Are People Paid?

There are three particular ways that people can be paid in an affiliate marketing campaign. These vary based on what is being offered. The type of payment options that a merchant offers to affiliates should be analyzed based on the values, and how you can qualify to receive them:

1. Traditional Commissions

A traditional commission would simply be a percentage of the sale. For instance, you might get 50 or 60 percent of the sale that you generate by your referral. This is the most commonly utilized type of commission.

2. Cost-Per-Action

The cost-per-action option refers to a situation where a merchant pays the affiliate for each acquisition. For instance, a merchant might pay an affiliate for each click onto a site or for every time someone signs up for email messages. Merchants often use this for marketing because they know they do not have to pay for anything unless they can actually get people to buy or sign up for whatever they have to offer.

3. By-the-Product Sales

By-the-product sales refer to when very specific physical items are purchased from a site. Instead of being valued based on a percentage of the sale, your payment is a set amount based on the type of product you help sell. This often works in cases where large items for sale are being promoted. For instance, if you forwarded a person to a site that sells vacuum cleaners, you might receive a commission of $75 for each vacuum that a person buys from your link. This could work for any type of vacuum that qualifies for the sale.

These three options for getting paid are different but they can all be profitable. The amount of money you earn as an affiliate depends on the effort you put into the program.

Be certain you know what to expect in the way of payments when you get your campaign up and running. Additional information on how payments can be provided to you will be covered in a later chapter in this guide. This includes details on some special and intriguing ways to receive even more money.

What Do Merchants Want From Affiliates?

Anyone can be an affiliate for any merchant. This is the true beauty of affiliate marketing. You do not have to have prior experience. However, merchants these days are very selective when choosing affiliates. They want those affiliates to meet a few standards before they get into a campaign. Some of these standards include the following:

- You have to work within the particular niche in which the merchant works. You should know what it is when signing up and make sure that the site is easily accessible and listed well.

- You must be in a certain geographic market. Your merchant should let you know the specific types of people that will likely visit your site. In most cases, this would entail American traffic although, in some cases, British and Canadian traffic may be considered.

- Your ability to promote various things offered by the merchant is vital. Some merchants ask you to work with just one product. Others require you to highlight several items, including some that might only be available for a brief time.

- Web 2.0 technology is also a requirement. Merchants often require their affiliates to work with social networks, blogs, and other ways of interacting with the online world to produce distinct static content.

Every program has its own needs and demands. Be sure you know the standards for your program when finding a merchant to contact. Affiliate marketing is certainly an appealing option to consider when wanting to earn money from home. The functionality of making money is distinct and simple for all to follow.

As you will learn throughout this guide, affiliate marketing is a thrilling and exciting way to make money. Lots of things go into the process, though. You have to know how to handle them all and how to make your site more visible and useful if you wish to go places with your campaign.

Chapter 2: History of Affiliate Marketing

Affiliate marketing is a unique process. While it has become very popular in the online world, it goes well beyond that and its origins lie elsewhere. Affiliate marketing has been continually growing and working well thanks to the simple layout that it utilizes. This has been refined over the years and continues to evolve as one of the top options utilized by anyone looking to make money online.

The Early Days

Affiliate marketing has been around in some form or another for generations. Its basic concept has been repeated by many groups over the years. It is not fully clear when the concept of affiliate marketing first started but we do know that people have been using it in some form for years. A referral is a case in point - a business that provides people with a reward if they refer others to that business.

For instance, you might have been asked by an auto mechanic after getting an oil change to refer him to a friend. You might then tell someone about becoming a new client at that mechanic's garage. That new customer would have to tell the mechanic that you recommended the mechanic's services to him or her. The mechanic would then provide you with a reward because you referred a new customer to his business. This might be a special discount on the next oil change or some other special benefit. Whatever the case, you will get some kind of reward for the referral. The practice is a tried and true routine that continues to be utilized by businesses to this day. This is especially true of businesses in smaller communities that cater to locals' needs.

Naturally, the online world has made this form of referral marketing a little easier to use. Today, cookies and browser memory information can help different types of marketing campaigns work right. The world of Web 2.0 also ensures that people can quickly enter the affiliate marketing field.

Getting Online

The online world has made it easier for people to get in touch with one another for business purposes. However, it was not until 1989 that affiliate marketing became prominent. That year, William J. Tobin set up his own affiliate marketing program through his PC Flowers and Gifts website. He set up a program with the Prodigy Network so he could get his flowers and gifts sold online. Prodigy was an online service portal that helped people get online and utilize various tools and activities through a secure connection.

The Prodigy Network would link people up to his products and provide revenue to Tobin and his business. In exchange, Prodigy would get a sizable cut of the sales that came about through its services. In 1996, Tobin successfully applied for a patent on the tracking and affiliate marketing process. This was a result of his idea of mainstreaming the concept of making affiliate marketing available to the general public. Of course, this refers in particular to the online aspect of marketing and how it can be utilized.

Tobin's effort was vital in helping people understand how well affiliate marketing could work. Countless others looked to find connections by which they could make their products more visible based on what Tobin had done with his company. This led to one of the most prominent online retailers in the world getting in on the action – Amazon.

Amazon Gets in

The efforts of PC Flowers and Gifts to make affiliate marketing a more viable endeavor were important. It was not until the mid-1990's that the practice really started to take off. As the online world continued to evolve, it became easier for people to track others with cookies.

The development of tracking cookies made it possible for a company to use as many affiliates as it wanted. Instead of having to stick with just one entity in the marketing process, a business could get several affiliates to promote its wares. The business could distinguish each affiliate based on the cookies that are read in the referral process.

This eventually led to Amazon.com producing its own affiliate marketing program. The site had been growing as it evolved from just selling books to selling more media products. It was on the way to becoming the retail juggernaut it is today but even then it was innovative. The new marketing program that Amazon was about to create was proof of how viable such a program could be.

Amazon.com created a special program that would provide people with money for promoting the site. The Amazon Associates Program was established with a simple design where the public could help promote what Amazon had to offer. This program allowed anyone who had a personal website to create a box that linked up to Amazon. That box could even include information on products available for sale on that site. Each box also included a link to the site or to a particular product page.

When a customer clicked on that Amazon link from a personal site, he or she received a tracking cookie that specified information on how that person got onto Amazon. When the customer bought something, a percentage of the sale would go to the site on which the link was posted.

This process is simple and easy to utilize. In fact, you might notice that to this day many websites have Amazon boxes that feature details on products available for sale. These websites can still get commissions from sales generated by people who access Amazon through those links. In fact, sometimes a link could be embedded directly into the text of whatever is on the site. People can even choose to have particular products listed on their Amazon boxes instead of using random ones, thus increasing their chances for producing sales. In other cases, people can choose to have those Amazon boxes show items relating to what is popular at a time or what a person had been looking for on the site in the past.

The most important aspect of the program is that this opened up the world of affiliate marketing to the public. In the early days of the internet, only businesses could get their affiliate programs running. As more people had the power to create their own websites and blogs, it became easier for them to produce unique content. The Amazon program is still working to this very day. In fact, you will learn a little more about it in a later chapter in this guide.

The Development of Networks

The first major affiliate networks started up in 1998, when ClickBank and Commission Junction were introduced. These were networks designed to provide businesses with an opportunity to get in touch with people who want to be affiliates. These network sites allowed a business to post information on a marketing opportunity online and affiliates to sign up to get into these marketing programs.

A network would then receive a portion of the sales generated by these affiliate links. This is a simple process that is easy to use and easy to benefit from. The most important part of this development is that it became easier for smaller retailers to offer their own affiliate campaigns. Businesses no longer had to be as large as Amazon to have their own programs. Just look at the ClickBank website today and you will see that the businesses associated with it come in many forms and from various industries.

Such campaigns can also be fully customized, thus improving how businesses could augment their affiliates' efforts. They can prepare their own graphics, set their own standards for how people are paid, and so forth.

The Growth of Blogging

In the past, people could only get affiliate marketing to work for them by creating their own personal websites. While anyone can still do this, the growth of blogging and social media has made it easier for people to get into particular marketing programs. As the Web 2.0 world continues to expand, it becomes easier for people to get online and create their own bits of content. This has helped affiliate marketing campaigns to grow.

Anyone can create a quality blog or website online these days. It is easy to produce a site by using a simple website creator or blogging platform. The online world is truly a place where you can express your voice to the world. Best of all, there are no limits on what you can say when online. This makes it possible for you to promote anything you want there.

With such blogs and other features being prevalent, merchants can now create text links, advertising boxes in various sizes, and many other features to make marketing easier and for people and businesses to be more flexible in their marketing efforts. A blog could be focused on whatever is being marketed at any given time.

Affiliates can also use simple bits of code that may be added onto their websites. There is no need to use anything overly technical. Affiliates just have to cut and paste whatever is offered by the merchant and add it to their own website. The easy-to-use customization features of many website builders make it easy for affiliates to organize their links as they see fit. They can get their links out in spots that are very easy for people to find.

Affiliate marketing has also grown so that people can use multiple campaigns on their websites. In such cases, people can post three or four advertisements on their sites with each linking to different places to which they are affiliated. This works best when the affiliates are similar to one another in some manner.

The social media world made it easier for affiliate marketing efforts to grow. With social media, people can use distinct affiliate links that are organized right in the middle of their messages and posts. This adds to the variety of places from which people can get their messages out.

Affiliate marketing has truly evolved over the years and has become a very viable and intriguing form of earning money. It is impressive to see how this form of marketing has grown over time, and it is clear that it can only continue to thrive.

Made in the USA
Lexington, KY
10 May 2018